Ben & Me

Christmas 2010

Carole,

You will love
reading about old
Ben and will learn
much from his
beliefs and accomplishments.

We love you,

Pappa and Grandma

Merry Christmas 2010

Ben & Me

FROM TEMPERANCE TO HUMILITY

Stumbling Through Ben Franklin's Thirteen Virtues,
One Unvirtuous Day at a Time

CAMERON GUNN

A Perigee Book

A PERIGEE BOOK
Published by the Penguin Group
Penguin Group (USA) Inc.
375 Hudson Street, New York, New York 10014, USA
Penguin Group (Canada), 90 Eglinton Avenue East, Suite 700, Toronto, Ontario M4P 2Y3, Canada
(a division of Pearson Penguin Canada Inc.)
Penguin Books Ltd., 80 Strand, London WC2R 0RL, England
Penguin Group Ireland, 25 St. Stephen's Green, Dublin 2, Ireland (a division of Penguin Books Ltd.)
Penguin Group (Australia), 250 Camberwell Road, Camberwell, Victoria 3124, Australia
(a division of Pearson Australia Group Pty. Ltd.)
Penguin Books India Pvt. Ltd., 11 Community Centre, Panchsheel Park, New Delhi—110 017, India
Penguin Group (NZ), 67 Apollo Drive, Rosedale, North Shore 0632, New Zealand
(a division of Pearson New Zealand Ltd.)
Penguin Books (South Africa) (Pty.) Ltd., 24 Sturdee Avenue, Rosebank, Johannesburg 2196,
South Africa
Penguin Books Ltd., Registered Offices: 80 Strand, London WC2R 0RL, England

While the author has made every effort to provide accurate telephone numbers and Internet addresses at the time of publication, neither the publisher nor the author assumes any responsibility for errors, or for changes that occur after publication. Further, the publisher does not have any control over and does not assume any responsibility for author or third-party websites or their content.

First edition: September 2010

Library of Congress Cataloging-in-Publication Data

Gunn, Cameron.
    Ben & me : from temperance to humility : stumbling through Ben Franklin's thirteen virtues, one unvirtuous day at a time / Cameron Gunn.—1st ed.
        p.   cm.
    "A Perigee book."
    Includes bibliographical references.
    ISBN 978-0-399-53607-6
    1. Virtues.   2. Gunn, Cameron—Ethics.   3. Franklin, Benjamin, 1706–1790—Ethics.
4. Franklin, Benjamin, 1706–1790—Autobiography.   I. Title.   II. Title: Ben and me.
    BJ1521.G86 2010
    179'.9—dc22   2010012136

PRINTED IN THE UNITED STATES OF AMERICA

10 9 8 7 6 5 4 3 2 1

This book describes the real experiences of real people. The author has disguised the identities of some, but none of these changes has affected the truthfulness and accuracy of his story. Penguin is committed to publishing works of quality and integrity. In that spirit, we are proud to offer this book to our readers; however, the story, the experiences, and the words are the author's alone.

Most Perigee books are available at special quantity discounts for bulk purchases for sales promotions, premiums, fund-raising, or educational use. Special books, or book excerpts, can also be created to fit specific needs. For details, write: Special Markets, Penguin Group (USA) Inc., 375 Hudson Street, New York, New York 10014.

{CONTENTS}

{ACKNOWLEDGMENTS}

It is a surreal and daunting experience to acknowledge the many people I need to thank for their help, directly or indirectly, in producing this book. It is my first published book. Maybe it will be my only one. What if I miss someone and I never get the chance to correct the error in another book? And what order do I do this in? Will people be offended if they're not first . . . or last, for that matter? I'm feeling a lot of pressure. It is only my sincere appreciation for their efforts that compels me to continue.

First, Chris Levan. This book was a two-person effort. Chris's guidance, his modern take on Franklin's virtues, and his encouragement helped create *Ben & Me*. When it was apparent that there were two books in *Ben & Me*—my stumbles through Franklin's virtues and Chris's weekly guide for my efforts—Chris's graciousness in letting me publish mine first completed the birthing process. Thanks, Chris.

My agent, Carolyn Swayze, took a flier on me with my first mystery novel. Without her patience and persistence in trying to find someone else to take a chance on me, I wouldn't be writing this acknowledgment. You're the best, Carolyn! (Thanks also to Kris Rothstein.)

In Marian Lizzi, super-editor, Carolyn found a kindred spirit and lover of Benjamin Franklin. Her patience helped guide me gently through a process that was completely alien to me. I'm sure it was occasionally painful and frustrating, but she never made it seem so. I wish for every author an editor like Marian—and her super-assistant, Christina Lundy.

To those who reviewed this text, Hilary Drain, Jade Spalding, and Don MacPherson (and Mom, but she gets her own mention later), your words of wisdom, grammatical suggestions, and encouragement helped make this book a reality. Thank you.

I talked to a bunch of people during the thirteen weeks and after about the various virtues. You'll see their names scattered throughout the book, so I won't repeat them here. Thanks to all of you for your help and direction.

What can I say about Leland and Faye Gunn? I know everybody says that they have the best parents in the world, but they're lying because I have the best parents in the world. They taught me right from wrong.

Life can be tough, whether you're trying to be a better person or just trying to get through the day. It helps to have great partners. I've got the greatest. My wife, Michelle, and my children, Kelsey, Harper, and Darcy, make my life, virtuous or not, special and interesting. This book is dedicated to them.

The Wife, the Sloth, and Virtuous Ben

I AM A SLOTH.

Or so says my wife.

In a moment of mental weakness, I asked my spouse about her perceptions of me: good qualities, bad qualities, areas for improvement. The animal thing was a throwaway—a little humor to lighten the mood. *If I were an animal, what would I be?* That's when she hit me with sloth. My companion to the grave thinks of me as a tree-hanging herbivore.

Maybe, I told myself, she had mistaken the sloth for another animal. Bright as she is, she's no zoologist. Did she know that up to two-thirds of a sloth's body weight consists of the contents of its stomach? Did she know that a sloth can muster the ambition to poop and pee only once a week? Did she know

{ *He is ill clothed that is bare of virtue.* }

that their only real defense is to move so slowly that predators miss them altogether, walking right past without even noticing?

Surely she meant to say shark . . . or stallion. I'd have taken stallion in a heartbeat.

"Why?" I asked, clearly compounding my earlier error. "Why a sloth?"

"Well, maybe not a sloth," Michelle answered. I said a quiet, prayerful thank-you before she continued. "Maybe a hippopotamus."

I blame Benjamin Franklin for all of this.

How could anyone blame good old Ben? After all, Franklin is the one figure of American history that seems so unabashedly *unblameworthy*. Inventor, scientist, diplomat, politician, soldier, and, of course, printer. A Revolutionary Renaissance man.

Friendly and affable, Franklin charmed kings and commoners, loyalists and revolutionaries. As a diplomat, he excelled at emulating, to his advantage, the backwoods gentleman. He started a long and successful career as a writer by passing anonymous letters to his unsuspecting publisher brother in the guise of a sharp-tongued widow. His most famous accomplishment as an inventor (or philosopher, as scientists of the day were called) came through the use of a kite. How can you not like someone who conducts experiments by flying kites? He is, as biographer Walter Isaacson has said, the Founding Father "who winks at us."[1]

So how was this brilliant, quirky visionary implicated in my wife's matter-of-fact stomp on my ego? Ironically, it was my discovery of Ben's struggles to become a better person that led to this moment of domestic disharmony. That and what I call the "Triple T" syndrome.

I am a living, breathing example of the Triple T syndrome. Were you able to see me, you would notice two things about my physical appearance. First, my hair is *Thinning* (that's T No. 1). Once endowed with thick, wavy tresses, I am now a victim of one of life's cruel ironies. With each passing day, a few more hairs fall from my scalp to the shower floor. They are, metaphorically, the dropping of the blooms of my youth—a visceral reminder that my time is passing. I'm not sure of the female equivalent to Thinning. I might guess the "change of life," but that doesn't start with a T, and I'm liable to be swarmed by emails from perimenopausal women enraged that I'd compare their state of hormone-induced agony to the relative insignificance of a few missing follicles. In any event, as my hair goes, so, I am reminded, goes my time on this mortal coil.

A glance down my frame reveals T No. 2: a *Thickening* of my waist (I actually spelled that *waste* at first—a nice Freudian slip). With each new dawn, I seem to take up a larger portion of the universe. I am not alone, of course, in this matter of my appearance. On this continent, our level of girth has become an epidemic. I'm sure you've seen the same statistics as I have that suggest that over half of all Americans are overweight. They are usually displayed on some chart with a graphic of a little silhouette man with love handles and a potbelly. Sadly, that's me. Another reminder of T No. 2: I can't run like I once could. I get tired just watching basketball games now. I am less attractive than I was in my youth (in my case, this is truly unfortunate since I was starting that particular race from a long way back in the pack). I could be William Shatner's body double (give or take a few inches off the top). I am Thickening and Thinning; I am more and less than I once was.

If the first two T's seem like harbingers of doom, it is the third T that offers a glimmer of hope—false, battle-scarred, unreasonable hope, but hope nonetheless. The third T is *Thirsting*. In the face of the first two T's—with their foretaste of aging and waning prowess, with their glimpse into the maw of mortality, with their backhand to the cheek of youthful promise—we seek to achieve before it is too late. It is these first two T's that feed the last. We (read "I" in this case) see that our lives are finite, we feel our strength ebb, and we know that the time to make our mark on the world draws short. We are a beagle on its morning walk—we long to pee on the tree of life to mark our passing. We thirst to be better, to be more, to be "something." Like Marlon Brando, we long to be a contender.

Perhaps that is how I discovered Ben; my radar was up for fellow Thirsters. As I scanned the newsstand one day, I spotted Franklin's face on the cover of *Time* magazine. In the article, "Citizen Ben's Great Virtues," Walter Isaacson describes Franklin this way:

> Through his self-improvement tips for cultivating personal virtues and through his civic-improvement schemes for furthering the common good, he helped to create, and to celebrate, a new ruling class of ordinary citizens who learned to be tolerant of the varied beliefs and dogmas of their neighbors.[2]

Who knew? A "ruling class of ordinary citizens"? "The common good"? And what about these "self-improvement tips for cultivating . . . virtues"? For a Thirster, this appeared as an oasis in the desert.

Isaacson goes on to caution that "the lessons from Franklin's life are more complex than those usually drawn by either his fans or his foes. Both sides too often confuse him with the striving pilgrim he portrayed in his autobiography." With that warning, he throws out a challenge—an invitation, if you will, to more closely examine "Citizen Ben":

> It is useful for us to engage anew with Franklin, for in doing so we are grappling with a fundamental issue: How does one

live a life that is useful, virtuous, worthy, moral and spiritually meaningful?[3]

So I took up the invitation. I researched, I surfed the web, and I read books. Most important, I discovered Franklin's autobiography. Started in 1771 as a series of letters intended for his son, William, Franklin wrote a remarkably readable chronicle of his life. Along with musings on science, literature, and philosophy, Franklin described a course of self-improvement he devised when he

{ Each year one vicious habit discarded, in time might make the worst of us good.}

was a young man. It was a "bold and arduous project of arriving at moral perfection." Franklin's stated rationale was a desire to "live without committing any fault at any time." You may call him delusional, but you can't fault his ambition.

Franklin's course required him to focus, for a week at a time, on a particular virtue. There were thirteen virtues in total. After a week, he would go on to the next virtue until he had completed the entire course. Each virtue was accompanied by an explanation, or "precept," as he called them. In truth, and in the harsh light of almost three hundred years of hindsight, the "precepts" look more like "outs." Chastity, for instance, didn't mean "no sex." To Franklin, it meant "rarely use venery but for health or offspring, never to dullness, weakness, or the injury of your own or another's peace or reputation." That's a pretty wide-open virtue. Probably a good thing, too; a course of self-improvement that included a complete prohibition on sex would have a very small market—monks, nuns, and maybe some diehard *Star Trek* conventioneers.

The list of virtues reads like an ethical dinner menu:

1. **Temperance:** Eat not to dullness; drink not to elevation.

2. **Silence:** Speak not but what may benefit others or yourself; avoid trifling conversation.

3. **Order:** Let all your things have their places; let each part of your business have its time.

4. **Resolution:** Resolve to perform what you ought; perform without fail what you resolve.

5. **Frugality:** Make no expense but to do good to others or yourself, i.e., waste nothing.

6. **Industry:** Lose no time; be always employed in something useful; cut off all unnecessary actions.

7. **Sincerity:** Use no hurtful deceit; think innocently and justly, and if you speak, speak accordingly.

8. **Justice:** Wrong none by doing injuries or omitting the benefits that are your duty.

9. **Moderation:** Avoid extremes; forbear resenting injuries so much as you think they deserve.

10. **Cleanliness:** Tolerate no uncleanliness in body, clothes, or habitation.

11. **Tranquillity:** Be not disturbed at trifles, or at accidents common or unavoidable.

12. **Chastity:** Rarely use venery but for health or offspring, never to dullness, weakness, or the injury of your own or another's peace or reputation.

13. **Humility:** Imitate Jesus and Socrates.

Franklin's "moral perfection" project is not without its critics. Micki McGee, author of *Self-Help, Inc.: Makeover Culture in American Life*,[4] suggests that Franklin was the progenitor of the modern self-help movement—our cultural obsession with single-handedly making ourselves "better." The self-help bookshelves groan with advice on how to be happy, how to handle sadness, how to maximize potential, how to minimize stress. Articles abound on how to overcome anxiety, depression, panic, mother issues, father issues, and just about every other kind of issue you can think of. Materials on self-esteem seem to be very popular, though I can't help wondering if being seen with a book on how to build self-esteem is good for self-esteem. "Coping" is also a popular theme: cope with difficult parents, cope with difficult kids, cope with difficult employers, cope with difficult employees. I imagine that somewhere there are two people sitting on opposite sides of a wall reading books on how to cope with each other.

The self-help industry churns out multimedia fixes for everything, usually with catchy titles and blue-sky promises. There are motivational speakers and business speakers, life coaches and self-esteem gurus. They scream at you from infomercials and smile at you from promotional cutouts. They practically plead with you to recognize how pathetic you've been and how only they can help. Embrace success (they scream!): All for only three easy payments of $29.95. Money-back guarantee if not completely satisfied. Some restrictions may apply.

SO WHY IS IT THAT SO MANY SEEM COLLECTIVELY SO ENAMORED OF these "programs"? Why do books on self-improvement and programs of personal empowerment seem to capture our imagination and our wallets? Some commentators have said it is a result of our narcissism. Others claim that it is some combination of the twin philosophies of empowerment and victimization. I think there are just a lot of Triple T sufferers. Remember Thinning, Thickening, and Thirsting?

Whatever the reason, we buy books, we take courses, and we attend seminars. And we also fail. In *Sham: How the Self-Help Movement Made America Helpless*, Steve Salerno points out that the likeliest customer for a self-help book is someone who bought a similar book within the preceding eighteen months. "If what we sold worked," he says, "one would expect lives to improve. One would not expect people to need further help." [5]

Surely Benjamin Franklin, with his "arduous project of arriving at moral perfection," wasn't, as Micki McGee suggests, the father of such a dissolute and self-indulgent industry. He wasn't after profit or luxury. Franklin wasn't motivated by personal self-interest (okay, maybe a little). Though he may have desired financial security and personal achievement, history shows us that his was truly a quest for the common good.

He formed America's first lending library, a volunteer fire department, and a mutual insurance association. When he invented something with commercial potential, he refused to patent it so that it could be widely copied. He created a club for the exchange of political and philosophical ideas, and he promoted and practiced tolerance in matters of conscience and religion. The motto for his lending library was, "To pour forth benefits for the common good is divine." Citizen Ben was no self-help huckster.

In establishing his program of virtue, Franklin was simply trying to improve the lot of mankind by creating a habit of doing good in himself and others. Habit is a powerful thing. Habit is the bane of antismoking advocates and the boon of marketers. It is the spokes in the wheels of religion and commercialism and politics. It is the foundation of a successful exercise program and the gravestone of an unsuccessful diet. Cicero said, "Great is the power of habit. It teaches us to bear fatigue and to despise wounds and pain."[6] This was the power that Franklin sought to exploit to make himself and others better—a program for harnessing routine into a force for good. And he believed in it. As Isaacson notes, "His morality was built on a sincere belief in leading a virtuous life, serving the country he loved and hoping to achieve salvation through good works."[7]

And so, to return to the sloth, I blame Ben. For how can a person, a Thirster, who reads of Franklin's virtues not seek to emulate him? Franklin issued that very challenge when he wrote of his course, "I hope, therefore, that some of my descendants may follow the example and reap the benefit."

Now, if you knew me, as my wife, Michelle, does, you might be saying to yourself at this point, "Here we go again"; something sloth-like this way comes. John Hay once said of Theodore Roosevelt that if "you can restrain him for the first fifteen minutes after he has conceived a new idea," he would calm down and behave like a reasonable human being.[8] No one caught me before minute sixteen.

Who, I ask (rhetorically—no need for an answer here), needs more help seeking moral perfection than a scatterbrained lawyer? Who needs civic-minded intellectual hydration more than a chronic Thirster? Who should be more diligent in seeking virtues like Order and Resolution than an admitted procrastinator? Who requires help in seeking Justice if not a prosecutor? Who, I ask (a note of desperation creeping into my voice), needs more guidance than I?

So, I decided . . . no . . . I *resolved* to enter upon the course of virtue created and tried by this man of science, this inventor, this philosopher, this diplomat, this writer, this Founding Father.

That brings us back to the sloth. If I was going to do this, I wanted to be able to track my success—to see if I would truly be-

xviii THE WIFE, THE SLOTH, AND VIRTUOUS BEN

come a better man. So it was that I came to ask my wife (and others, whom you will meet shortly) to describe me so that I would know from whence I was starting. This is what social scientists call the baseline. With such an invitation, my wife called me a sloth. Well,

{ *Search others for their virtues, thyself for thy vices.* }

this tree-hanging, all-stomach, once-a-week-pooping (I hope you realize by now this is a metaphor), slow-moving sloth was set to follow in the footsteps of Benjamin Franklin. Thirteen weeks to moral perfection! The Founding Father's reputation and my own might not survive the effort.

The Preparations

*Either master the devil
or throw him out*

IF I WAS GOING TO SUCCEED AT FOLLOWING ONE OF HISTORY'S MOST
beloved characters on the path to moral perfection, then I needed a
plan. Actually, I thought I'd need a miracle, but I decided to start
with a plan.

Channeling my inner Sun Tzu, I decided I needed to understand the objective, the enemy opposing me, and the keys to victory.
But before I get too far ahead of myself, I think it best to begin the
entire program of virtue from a posi-
tion of honesty. I offer complete disclosure here—no room for half-truths or
hidden secrets. Let me deal with my
mea culpas up front. If one is to fight
the demon of mediocrity, one must at least acknowledge in which
foxhole one is cowering. Here goes.

{ *By failing to prepare,
you are preparing to
fail.* }

This was my fourth attempt at starting Franklin's course of virtues. You might have guessed from my use of the word "attempt" that I had never completed the course. I had not (in the previous three attempts) even progressed past the fifth virtue. That's three swings and not even a foul tip to show for my efforts. What does it say for my potential moral perfection that I had tried and failed three times? Too bad perseverance wasn't one of the virtues (or slothfulness—apparently I'd have that one wrapped up).

Indeed, my first try at Franklinism was never intended to be a matter of public record; it was a purely personal venture. I had no intention of writing about the experience. Heaven forbid that I should display my failures for all to see. After my first aborted attempt to remove vice from my life, however, I perceived the value in laying bare my soul (or at least my sins). If I was to fail, why not profit from my lack of achievement? Could greed be a catalyst to moral perfection? So I tried again and failed again. If I wasn't becoming morally perfect, at least I was gathering fodder for my literary efforts.

At some point, amid the wreckage of failed attempts, it became clear that I needed help. They say the first step is admitting you have a problem. First, as I mentioned above, I needed a plan—more on that later. But more than a plan, I needed some direct assistance. Virtue and ethics are not my bailiwick. I needed someone to lead me through the minefields of Franklin's virtues. I needed a guide, a sort of ethical sponsor. Of course I had Franklin, but I couldn't go to him for clarification or an explanation of how his course might translate to the modern world. I needed something more contemporary—a real live coach. I just had no idea who that could be.

And then I got drunk.

Sometime after Failed Attempt No. 3, I attended a work-related conference. There I was, away from home, among my peers, without responsibility. I did the opposite of what any man seeking a path to a more virtuous life should do: I went out with my friends and drank too much. A meal at a local pub with a colleague and a detective from the local police force led to a trip to another pub and then to the conference's hospitality suite. We made entirely too merry and I, as much as it pains me to admit it, was wholly intemperate. I struck a crushing blow to Franklin's first virtue. As is the way in this world, I paid for my vice the next morning.

One of the speakers at the conference was a friend of mine, Dr. Chris Levan, who is a writer, university professor, minister, and speaker in the areas of spirituality, professional ethics, and theology. He is the author of eight books on religion and moral values, and he has been the principal of St. Stephen's College in Edmonton, Alberta, and acting president of Huntington College. He's one of those spooky-smart people. Sometimes when we talk, he says things that go completely over my head. Then I have to decide if I should ask him what he's talking about or just nod, pretend I know what he means, and hope he doesn't ask any questions.

I had heard Chris speak on numerous occasions. Never, however, had I heard him in such an environment. This was a conference on preventing wrongful criminal convictions. I had no idea what Chris was doing there.

His talk, a general lecture on ethical decision making, was a tough pitch. The audience at this conference was almost exclusively made up of police officers and prosecutors. The theme of the conference, and the impetus for it, already had many in the audience spoiling for a fight. The premise underlying the whole event was that there had been a number of people wrongfully convicted and jailed and that it was somehow law enforcement's fault. Our brothers and sisters in arms had screwed up, and we were going to be told (generally by people with no frontline experience in the criminal justice system) how not to screw up in the future. Tough crowd. Some with guns.

To deliver a successful talk, you have to know your audience and pick your topic, speaking style, and message carefully. Chris started his speech to jaded police and prosecutors by showing them a painting by Rembrandt. It was, I thought, courageous. Strange, but courageous. Don't ask me what the painting represented.

By the end of his talk, despite the audience's misgivings, he had this hardened group of law enforcement officials enthralled. He had them considering the mechanics of ethical decisions through the use of classic artwork. It occurred to me—flaunter of Franklin's virtues, intemperate soul, and failed moral perfectionist—that I had found my sponsor. Thus, in the wake of intemperance, the good ship *Morally Perfect* was about to set sail . . . again (with a better captain and crew this time).

Chris wasn't prepared to sign on without some idea of what I was trying to do. He asked, "What do you want people to get out of this book?" It was a reasonable question, and it deserved a cogent and thoughtful answer. If I was capable of that, however, I wouldn't need a course dedicated to moral perfection (or at least I would have passed it on one of my first three attempts).

Of course, I wanted the book to be about my attempts to follow Benjamin Franklin's list of virtues, but that was a premise, not a goal, and I was sure that Chris wanted specifics. He wanted to know what benefit, specifically, readers would gain from following my quest. Still, I had nothing.

Perhaps if I couldn't answer what I wanted the book to be, I could tell him what I knew it would *not* be.

First, this was not to be, and is not, a history book or a biography of Benjamin Franklin. Except for Ben's autobiography and other writings, I have relied almost exclusively on secondary and tertiary sources for my information about good ol' Ben. I have done no independent research, analytical study, or even critical examination of the sources I have relied on. The basis of my knowledge of American history comes largely from *Schoolhouse Rock*, those catchy educational cartoons on Saturday morning television in the 1970s (if you know the tune to "But I know I'll be a law someday, / At least I hope and pray that I will, / But today I am still just a bill," then you know what I'm talking about). Let me repeat: This is not a book of history; most sixth-grade students would know more about Benjamin Franklin than I do. (At this point I should acknowledge that I am Canadian. That might make me even less qualified to write about an American icon, but knowing my nationality might help readers understand the reason an occasional hockey or lumberjack reference pops up.)

Likewise, no analytical scholarship will have wheedled its way into the pages of this text; as I said above, my sources are largely secondary, and I rely on the Internet more than an online Texas Hold 'em addict.

Nor is this a book of philosophy, religion, or spirituality. My credentials to speak on any of the above topics are decidedly scanty; I dropped first-year philosophy when I learned that there was a mathematical component, I almost got kicked out of my religious confirmation class for acting up, and you wouldn't get your ankles wet wading in the pool of my spiritual knowledge. Indeed, you will find nothing in this book that advocates following a particular creed, religious doctrine, or any form of theological thinking. Franklin himself, as best I can understand it, believed in a higher power but not in dogmatic religion.

This is not a book that contains answers to the fundamental questions of existence. Arthur Herman, author of *How the Scots Invented the Modern World*, poses the question, "How do human beings become moral beings, who treat one another with kindness, regard and cooperation, rather than brutality and savagery?"[1] Good question. If you were expecting an answer to such a question in the pages of this book, you were mistaken. I have no qualifications, professional credentials, or history of past successes that might make me a candidate for offering advice on how to be a better person. I'll leave that to Ben.

{ *'Tis easier to prevent bad habits than to break them.*}

Finally, this was not to be a book of great adventures or extravagant gestures. If I was to achieve anything, it had to be consistent with how Ben would have approached things. His was a course of daily living, not a journey up Everest.

At this point, you're probably asking yourself (as I'm sure my friend Chris was) if there is anything of value to be found in this book. Having spelled out what it is not, perhaps I had better give some idea of what this book *is* (or rather what I *hope* it is).

This is a diary of frequent failure and rare success. It is the account of one man's largely unsuccessful attempts at self-improvement through emulating one of history's giants. It is the journal of a quest. It is a tale for Thirsters. That's it. Nothing more.

Let's get on with the preparations.

Franklin's Course

To understand Franklin's course (and thus to replicate it), one must understand Franklin. He was clearly, in the language of twenty-first-century management courses, goal oriented; one does not discover electricity or invent the armonica (no, there is no *h* missing from this word—look it up!) without good project management skills. In fact, his course has all the features of a well-planned venture: a defined goal, a daily task list, and a method for measuring success.

To ensure a daily compliance to the project, he developed what must have been the world's first day planner. He allotted times to all his business and assigned himself the task of conceiving a "good deed" day. Here's an example from his autobiography:

The Morning Question, What good Shall I do this Day?	5 6 7	Rise, wash, and address *Powerful Goodness*; Contrive day's good shall I do this Business, and take the resolution of the day; prosecute the present Study: and breakfast?—
	8 9 10 11	Work
	12 1	Read, or overlook my Accounts, and dine.
	2 3 4 5	Work.
	6 7	Put Things in their Places, Supper,
Evening Question, What Good have I done to day?	8 9	Musick, or Diversion, or Conversation, Examination of the Day.
	10 11 12 1 2 3 4	Sleep.—

Of course, Franklin felt the need to track his successes and failures. To do so, he created a graph, recognizable to first graders everywhere as the "Gold Star" chart. Instead of rewards for good deeds, however, he marked down each transgression of the virtues. Here's how he described it:

> I made a little book, in which I allotted a page for each of the virtues. I rul'd each page with red ink, so as to have seven columns, one for each day of the week, marking each column with a letter for the day. I cross'd these columns with thirteen red lines, marking the beginning of each line with the first letter of one of the virtues, on which line, and in its proper column, I might mark, by a little black spot, every fault I found upon examination to have been committed respecting that virtue upon that day.

In his autobiography he showed the form of the pages:

TEMPERANCE

EAT NOT TO DULLNESS; DRINK NOT TO ELEVATION.							
	S	M	T	W	Th	F	Sat
Temperance							
Silence	★	★		★		★	
Order	★★	★	★		★	★	★
Resolution			★			★	
Frugality		★			★		
Industry			★				
Sincerity							
Justice							
Moderation							
Cleanliness							
Tranquillity							
Chastity							
Humility							

Finally, despite the project's secular context, Ben did not discount the hand of providence or the effect of inspiration. Among several mottos, prayers, and credos that he would recite daily to get over the hurdles was one he composed himself:

O powerful Goodness! bountiful Father! merciful Guide!
increase in me that wisdom which discovers my truest interest.
Strengthen my resolutions to perform what that wisdom dictates.
Accept my kind offices to thy other children as the only return
in my power for thy continual favors to me.

Oh, how I like the way that Ben's mind worked. So practical and pragmatic; so focused on the goal. And yet for all his practicality he was a dreamer of the first order. This practical, yet wistful, approach to the program offered real opportunity for an acolyte such as me. I could copy the "tools" that Ben used in his quest. Thus, in preparation for stumbling after Ben, I created my own virtuous day planner and progress chart—a modern equivalent of Franklin's little book. I call it the Virtue Tracker™. Maybe I'll market it for those intrepid souls foolhardy enough to follow in the wake of both Franklin and me. (The Virtue Tracker™ is not really trademarked. This was just an attempt to be funny. Forgive me—I suppose it's a bit of lawyer humor.)

So I had the book, its virtue-tracking pages clean and ready to record my transgressions. Within its pages were the very poems Ben used to inspire himself. But just buying a toolbox does not make you a carpenter. Or is that a tool belt?

If Franklin's course is about changing and creating habits, replacing the bad with the good, then I next decided that I must know who I am. I must know from whence I am starting this particular journey. I call this section . . .

. . . The Good, the Bad, and the Ugly

It is difficult to be introspective. I am reminded every time I see a picture of myself or hear my voice on a recording that my own self-image is not consistent (even in superficial ways) with how others see me (or, more important, with reality). I decided, in preparing for this course, to begin by making things easy on myself and to let others begin the process. What do those around me think of me? I decided to take a survey.

That's where the sloth thing came up. It was not a promising start.

I came up with some very unscientific questions as I sat on the couch and interviewed my wife (while watching TV, mind you). Immediately thereafter I lost both my questions and her answers.

Make a mark under "Disorganized." Maybe I was traumatized by the sloth comment. Perhaps it just hit too close to the bone. Or possibly as a male, I am unable to watch TV and carry on a conversation at the same time.

{ *How few there are who have courage enough to own their faults, or resolution enough to mend them.* }

I soon regrouped and re-created the survey from memory. Essentially I asked the participants to rate me relative to Franklin's virtues and then list my good and bad qualities (I did pose the animal question to all—once I got sloth, I assumed it could get no worse). In order to lessen the blow to my ego, I'll reproduce my email to my parents along with their responses (a good rule of thumb: If you are going to reveal your character to the world, start off with your mother's assessment). Here it is:

1. Please make a list of my good and bad qualities (honesty is required).

2. If I were an animal, what animal would I be?

3. Please consider the 13 virtues (I listed them) as described by Benjamin Franklin, and rate me on a scale of 1 to 10, 10 being the best.

That's it. Thanks and don't forget to be honest.

And now the answers (from, mind you, the two people who gave me life, raised me, and saw me off into the world. I should also acknowledge that I am their only child):

We were not too smart with the virtues, Benjamin was too sophisticated for us; not sure we understood them. Any way here goes.

Good Qualities—Honest, loyal, intelligent, easygoing, great memory, proud, kind, fair, compassionate, interested in everything, a leader, a teacher, great father and son, very much a family man, curious, happy, content with lot in life, ambitious for the right things, listens to his mother (joke). Someone must have brought you up right, ha. Perfect sunny boy or is it Sunshine And Lollipops.

Faults—Has difficulty saying no and asking for help, not sure that is a fault. Picks at his nose, doesn't tie his shoelaces. Sometimes forgets he is not in the Court Room and interrogates his wife.

Newfoundland Dog because he is lumbering, friendly and happy, strong and may have descended from The Vikings as did the Gunns.

Virtues—1, 2, 3, 4, 5, 6, 10, 11, 13 were a 9 and the rest a 10, we are not sure about Socrates' teachings.

Mom and Dad

Ha! Take that, Michelle! A Newfoundland dog is scarcely what I want written on my tombstone, but it was a whole lot better than sloth. How can you not start off the day with a song in your heart and a smile on your face when you know that your parents regard you in such a way?

About now, you are probably having the same concerns as I was.

As warm and fuzzy as my parents' survey made me feel, they are not the most objective observers. A note of neutrality was required. It was time to move on to other participants.

I decided to try coworkers and friends. I should have quit while I was ahead. Their assessment was far less biased (and far more realistic). A coworker described me as honest and principled but egocentric and scatterbrained. The friend I had chosen refused to respond.

In the end, it was apparent to me that I was only engaging in procrastination. The most important assessment had to be my own. I had asked others who I was (in the context of Franklin's specific virtues), but no one knows me like I do—kinda.

So here we go. As Oliver Cromwell said, "Paint me warts and all."

I am, if I am being forthright, egotistical but sometimes suffer from low self-esteem. I am smart but not nearly as smart as I suppose. I speak well but do so before I think. I am impulsive but overly cautious in some of life's most important decisions. My use of money is not frivolous, but I have accumulated no wealth in forty years on the earth. I love sports and exercise, but not as much as I love food; the result is a waistline that grows ever so slightly each year. The words "order" and "organization" invoke in me a sense of dread—a notion of something Orwellian. My wife describes me as a Boy Scout (except when it comes to manual tasks). I have a sense of what is right and wrong, and on occasion, I, too, rigidly adhere to that code (read uptight). Patience is probably my greatest virtue and arrogance my worst vice. In short (has this been short?), I am like most other people: I am a bag of contradictions, constantly changing and evolving.

As I read the list over, I am struck by one notion: It's not as bad as I suspected. But that's only half the equation. This is a book about change, a journey of self-improvement. So the next question, the destination for this book, was: *Who do I want to be?* Chris, my new ethical guide, suggested that a useful way to pose the question is: *What do you want people to be saying as you die?*

Frankly, I want them to say: *Isn't there anything else we can do to save him?*

But assuming all heroic measures have been taken and my time is past, I think that I just want to be remembered. That may seem simple, but it seems to me that life's purpose is to first live (in the fullest sense) and then to leave some sort of legacy. Maybe that's just vanity, but in the spirit of honesty, that is what I think. So how about this: *He was a wonderful father, husband, and son. He saw things, went places, and, most important, he made a difference.* Is that simple enough?

Could Ben help me with these rather vague but universal goals? Well, we'll see. Each week, for thirteen weeks, I would concentrate on the virtues that made Benjamin Franklin America's most beloved son. I would be Temperate and Sincere and Moderate. I'd attempt to carry out Justice and practice Cleanliness. When I didn't understand what these things meant, I'd seek direction. (Chris Levan had agreed to write a twenty-first-century translation of each virtue, some of which I'll share with readers.) Along the way, I hoped to find some answers as to why we do this—why we constantly seek to *improve*.

Armed, then, with some sense of myself, an ethical guide, and a homemade copy of Ben's day planner and progress chart, I stepped, tentatively, forward. So began my journey—my humble attempt to follow a course of virtuous behavior invented 250 years before my birth. I had no preconceived notions of where this journey would take me, nor was I deluded about my potential level of virtuousness at its conclusion.

In truth, I had no idea what I was doing or where I was going.

CHAPTER 1

Temperance

Eat not to dullness;
drink not to elevation

OH DEAR.

I had visions of such promise with this whole endeavor. It would be a walk through the proverbial park. How tough could it be to follow a course of virtues that included things like Tranquillity? Sit under a tree reading a book and I'm already a master's candidate. Perhaps I should have paid more attention to the order of the virtues.

Franklin's choice of Temperance as Virtue No. 1 was no accident. Temperance would be easy for a man who had already decided against excessive drinking or eating. But what about those of us for whom excess is a hobby?

{ I guess I don't so much mind being old, as I mind being fat and old.}

I am not Ben Franklin, as we've already established. Temperance, for me, is not easy. This is not the virtue I would have picked to start things off with. I might not normally be intemperate in drink, but I am a candidate for a twelve-step program when it comes to food. I've been trying since I was a boy not to "eat to dullness," and yet dull I am. If the idea was to start with a virtue that would establish a pattern of success, Justice or Cleanliness would have been a nice beginning. But Temperance!?

Of course, I was being too literal. In my friend Chris's instructions to me on this virtue he warned against such an interpretation. Franklin's view of Temperance, Chris indicated, is bound up more in his notions of usefulness and life's purpose than it is in his concern about overindulgence. He wrote (I swear I'm not making this up) that Franklin would have regarded Intemperance as slothful. Slothful! (I should rush to point out that Chris had no knowledge of Michelle's views on my animal doppelganger). Could this be just a coincidental use of the word by Chris? Would Franklin have actually used that word?

It turns out he did. Over and over again. He wrote, apparently, things like: "Diligence overcomes difficulties, sloth makes them," and "Sloth makes all things difficult, but industry, all things easy."

Whoa. Franklin abhorred sloth; I am, according to my wife, a sloth. I found more Franklin sloth quotes. Not surprisingly, none of them were in favor of it. I felt Franklin fixing me with his steely gaze across almost three hundred years of virtuous history. It was an inauspicious beginning, but let us return to Temperance.

The drinking I didn't anticipate to be a problem. I have a weekend beer and occasionally a drink after work on Friday with my coworkers, but except for a yearly golf trip and an annual get-together with work colleagues, I almost never drink to elevation. Of course, in college I majored in drinking to elevation, with a minor in leering, but I'm a long way from those days.

Food, on the other hand, is my nemesis. Ahab had his whale

(once again, that's a little Freudian), Superman his Lex Luthor. I have midnight snacks and trans fats. I am the "before" picture in the advertising campaign for exercise programs—the one that women at high school reunions are relieved "got away." My daughters call me "the Big Fat Teddy Bear." Clearly they have inherited their mother's tact.

Lest you think my dimensions are a recent problem, let me disabuse you of that notion. My weight is no middle-age albatross, shot with the arrow of a slowing metabolism and hung around the shoulders of paunchy adulthood. No, my corpulence is long-standing. It's a sad story really, one of those tales best told to therapists and self-help groups. "Hi, I'm Cameron, and I was a chunky kid."

I was a stout child. Childhood pictures of me show the progression of my intemperance. Chubby-faced infancy gave way, for all too brief a time, to childhood fitness, the product of a raging metabolism overcoming gluttony. By the time I was approaching adolescence, however, I was beginning to resemble Chunk from *The Goonies*. (If this is outside your cultural framework, go rent this movie and watch it with your family. You won't be disappointed.)

The dealers to my habit were my mother and my grandmother—wonderful, well-meaning women who displayed their love and affection through butter and sugar. For my grandmother (a woman who had a special dessert for each grandchild), it was cherry no-bake cheesecake. My mom's drug of choice was blueberry pie. If I close my eyes, I can still see the flaky crust clinging to the side of the glass pie plate, sweet, plump, freshly picked blueberries oozing up from any available crevice. In the middle of the pie there was a porcelain bird, its mouth open in eternal song, venting heat and, more important, scent and calling to me—my own personal siren urging me onto the rocks of overindulgence.

I'm not sure I knew that I was chubby when I was in elementary school. I should have recognized my condition in the fifth grade when the salesman at the local clothing store took one look at me and said, "I think he needs a husky size."

Husky. At the time I thought it was a compliment, an indication of an imposing physical presence. Only later did I understand that it was seventies clothing-salesman code speak for "fat." Sometimes being dim-witted is a blessing.

Neither dim-wittedness nor childhood delusions, however, could save me in junior high school. No, in that psychological torture chamber, that killer of the esteem of youth, it became apparent to me that "husky" was not a desirable physical characteristic in the minds of thirteen-year-old girls. I was beginning to become painfully aware of my size and shape. In gym class, I would try a host of tricks not to display myself to my classmates.

Somehow, despite my girth, I managed to play competitive hockey, volleyball, and, starting in the eighth grade, varsity basketball. I had not anticipated that it would necessitate me taking my clothes off in front of my teammates. No amount of trickery or gimmickry developed over the past year was going to allow me to maintain my "keep it covered" policy. And so there I was, bare to the world (or at least to twelve other teenage boys).

A ninth-grade student (who happened to play the same position as me, as I remember) noticed either my girth or my reluctance to change, or both, and decided to make me the object of scorn. He gave me the first nickname I can remember having. It was an ode to my size and my low shooting percentage (I was always a better rebounder than a shooter). It was to stick for some time. He called me "Fat Chance."

By high school, I had shed my boyhood fat. But I have remembered my first nickname. I have dragged that little scrap of memory with me into adulthood. In my mind, though I am now a husband, father, prosecutor, would-be author, and Benjamin Franklin emulator, there will always be a little "Fat Chance" in me.

So there it is. I approached this first virtue of Temperance with a history of self-indulgence. Maybe this was the perfect virtue with which to begin. Maybe I could start my moral perfection project with a little corporal improvement. After all, it was Franklin who said, "I guess I don't so much mind being old, as I mind being fat and old." Thus, notwithstanding Chris's instructions not to take things too literally and Ben's intentions, I decided to take the virtue of Temperance, at least in part, literally.

But how? It was not as if Ben left a menu planner and an exercise schedule along with his day planner. How could I turn Franklin's eighteenth-century virtue of Temperance into a twenty-first-century weight loss program?

I had no interest in a diet, being opposed to them based largely on a long-standing history of failure. More than that, however, they seem un-Franklinian. While they do follow the create-a-habit premise, they do it in an unsustainable way. Who, even if they manage to follow a diet for six weeks, is going to spend a lifetime eating nothing but oat bran, salmon, and lentils? No one! Not even the person who created the diet. Not even the mother of the guy who created the diet. "Oh, I'm very proud of Lionel. But lentils? Please, they make me bloat." No one follows a diet for the rest of their lives. Mostly, they follow them in short, miserable spurts. They feel horrible while they're on the diet, guilty when they go off of it, and then anxious when they start another one. It's all too much like a Dostoyevsky novel for me.

Finally, I decided on a simple plan that required no change in the diets of others; no support from friends, family, or coworkers; indeed, almost no change in how *I* eat. I resolved, as part of the Virtue of Temperance, not to eat between meals or eat after supper. My "diet" during Temperance Week (sounds like freshman week at a Bible college) was simple: I would not snack. That's it. Nothing else. (Well, I tried to eat more fruit, too, but that was just to set an example for the kids.)

There. Even I could follow such a program of Temperance. Of course, it was not earth-shattering nor did it deserve its own trademarked name; this was no OrganoPath or FiberFiesta. The program did, however, have the benefit of being achievable.

Having decided on a plan, I realized I needed a little mile marker on my virtuous journey. Food being my original sin, I needed to know to what level of Hell it had taken me. I don't often weigh myself—no one wants to be reminded that he is as heavy as a Smart car—but in the interests of my rush to moral perfection, I stood upon my electronic judge.

As I gazed down over my expanding middle, the little needle edged 250 pounds. I tried changing positions, sucking in, feeling lighter. No good; 250 it was—a depressing way to start a program of self-improvement. Why couldn't I have read a biography of William Howard Taft or Kirstie Ally?

Day 1: The Journey Begins

Maybe starting the program on a Monday wasn't a great idea. I probably shouldn't have sprung it on myself with so little notice. I went to bed a perfectly happy, if morally imperfect, man and woke up to the pressure of beginning a course of commitment that lasts longer than the NHL playoffs. The entire enterprise started wrong-footed. I had resolved to go back to my morning routine of dog walking but quickly fell into my alternative routine of hitting snooze on my alarm clock. By the time I got up, both the dog and I were disappointed with me.

The trick, I discovered from my last adventure with Ben, was not to let early failures get the best of me. Thus, I sat in the relative peace of my downstairs bathroom and read the poems of inspiration. Or in Franklin's words, I addressed Powerful Goodness! I'm not sure how Powerful Goodness felt being addressed from my porcelain perch, but with three children, several drop-ins my wife was looking after for the day, and a disappointed beagle nearby, it was the only private spot in the joint.

Notwithstanding my initial trepidation, I began to feel better about my chances. After all, Ben was trying to make this easy. He didn't say, "Abstain." He said, "Be Temperate." That's one of the things I like about Ben and his virtues—he gave himself an out with each one. He didn't even demand pure, unspoiled Temperance; he qualified his virtue. Don't eat so much you can't move, and if you drink, don't throw up on yourself. These are "virtue light"; I could do them.

And thus it began.

Upon my arrival at work, I was presented with an interesting opportunity to consider virtue and ethics in both a personal and a professional aspect. I spent most of the day dealing with people held in custody over the weekend: the sad, the bad, and the frequent flyers. From a strung-out twenty-year-old with hypodermic needles sewn into the lining of her coat, to two alcoholics caught up in their addictions, there were opportunities aplenty to consider the virtues of Temperance and Justice. The most ethically demanding, however, was an intellectually challenged man accused of a serious assault on a woman.

As the father of a special-needs child, I am acutely aware of the struggle between my duty as a prosecutor and my duty as a human being. I watched the man's elderly parents wait anxiously for his appearance and his own embarrassment as he glanced back at them, while his lawyer described the reasons why a mental health assessment was appropriate. At the conclusion of his bail hearing, the man was sent for a thirty-day assessment. Unfortunately, there were no spaces immediately available at the mental health facility, so he was to be sent to a jail to await transfer. Remembering Franklin (and thinking particularly of Justice), I alerted the jail to the accused's special needs and requested they segregate him for his own protection. Hardly a home run for virtue, as I was simply following my responsibility as a prosecutor, but it was at least a baby step down the road to moral perfection.

And the early victories for virtue continued. Not only was I working on the virtues but I was passing on the wisdom. One of my coworkers confided about a seething resentment (okay, maybe "seething" is strong, but I know she would say that she had every right to seethe) over the actions of a mutual acquaintance. It wasn't a new topic, so I came somewhat prepared. Remembering Franklin, and thinking particularly of Tranquillity (though in the moment I got it confused with Justice), I told her that life is a long road, and we are all drivers. If we choose to look at what has happened in the past, it is like looking in the rearview mirror; do it too often and you risk going off the road. Look ahead, I suggested, not back.

My colleague, a very bright professional woman with more than twenty years of experience in her field, shot me a look like she might a brazen child and then said, "That's not bad. I guess you're right."

Wooo hoooo! This Franklin thing was a breeze. Could it all be this easy? I am reminded here of the opening words of *Book the First* in *A Series of Unfortunate Events*: "If you are interested in stories with happy endings, you would be better off reading some other book."

One might think that being so occupied with Justice and Tranquillity would make the no-snacking/Temperance credo a breeze. One would be wrong.

All day long, despite the distractions, I had the fidgety, nervous twitches of someone in the grips of the DTs. I craved sugar . . . or salt . . . or starch. Maybe I didn't crave any of those things. Maybe I just craved snacking itself. Like a smoker dangling a wooden cigarette out of his mouth, maybe I'd be satisfied with some snack surrogate. I remember reading once that if you ate slowly, you could trick your body into believing it was full. Maybe I could do the same with snacks. Perhaps I could try to fool whatever compels me to snack by chewing on a straw or something. Of course, chewing on plastic can't be much better for me than overeating, but there is no censure against plastic consumption anywhere in Ben's autobiography. I decided it was worth a try.

The straws didn't work. I just had a bunch of chewed plastic in my wastebasket.

As I contemplated my straw failure and the merits of a snack in the midst of the day, I began to negotiate with myself. What could one little snack hurt? I reasoned. I can have just one. I can stop at any time.

What was I saying?

I'd gone from a generally happy, if slightly chubby and morally imperfect, person to a self-delusional food addict on Day 1 of my program. On a positive note, I was gaining a better understanding of the plight of the addicts in custody over the weekend.

If the workday had been daunting, the evening presented a distraction from my food struggles and an opportunity to flex my ethical muscles. I had managed to start my course of virtues not only nine days after Ben's three hundredth birthday but also on the date of Canada's federal election. This was not any old election, mind you, but a bitter, nasty, recrimination-filled slugfest between two ideologically opposite parties (actually, more than two parties run in a Canadian election, but much like the United States, there are only two that have a realistic hope of forming a government).

I had been, for the entire campaign, vacillating on my electoral choice. On Election Day, I was no closer to making a decision. By the time I came home from work, my wife had not only voted but told our two youngest daughters, five- and seven-year-olds, that she had cast her ballot for the local Green Party candidate (the Green Party is a small environmentally conscious party that garners no seats in parliament and less than 5 percent of the vote). She had told the girls that the reason she voted for a candidate she didn't know, from a party that she had barely heard of, was that they were the only party that had not run attack ads. I resisted, mindful of Franklin's dictate to "Speak not but what may benefit others or yourself," explaining that the absence of Green Party attack ads was a direct result of the absence of campaign finances, independent resources, and, indeed, the complete absence of Green Party ads of any sort.

After supper, I took my children with me to the polling station with the idea that it would be an excellent lesson in civics. I brought them both into the voting booth and showed them the ballot, explaining how one marked it. At this point, I still had not yet decided how I would vote.

Harper, the seven-year-old, looked at the ballot and said, "Vote for the Green Party. They're not mean like the other parties."

Now my first inclination was to say that there were better reasons to vote for people—strong public policy ideas, powerful leaders, economic considerations. But then it struck me: there was no better reason to vote for someone, at least not in this election. Green Party it was. I voted for a candidate I didn't know from a party that

I had barely heard of on the basis of how "not mean" they were. It felt strangely right.

Bringing this all back to Franklin, I initially felt pretty darn good. First, I had been industrious (always employed in something useful), and I had enough humility to recognize that a child could come up with as valid a reason as I for casting a ballot. However, my pleasure at being virtuous suffered an almost immediate double blow.

As we left the polling station, Harper asked, "Is that it?"

"Yes. That's it."

"That was no fun," she said, her voice tinged with disappointment.

Slightly taken aback but undaunted in my quest for virtue, I comforted myself with the fact that Darcy, the five-year-old, still seemed almost euphoric from the whole experience. She literally bounded to the car, not an unusual manner of stride for her. She maintained her positive disposition right up to the point that we left the parking lot and headed for our neighborhood.

"Where are we going?" she asked.

"Home," I replied.

There was pause before she asked, "But when do we go to the green party?"

At least I had been temperate at the polling station. It was a good thing they didn't supply snacks.

{ *In general, mankind, since the improvement of cookery, eats twice as much as nature requires.*}

The Struggle Begins Anew

My grandfather, used to years of waking at 4 a.m. to go to work in the mosquito-infested woods, would say about rising, "Put the palms of your feet on the floor and get ready to face the horrors of a new day." Inspiring stuff.

Notwithstanding the "horrors" that faced me, I was slightly more prepared for starting my second day as an acolyte of Ben. I addressed Powerful Goodness while drawn to my full height (as opposed to my bathroom conversation from Day 1) and prepared to meet the day in all its virtuous glory.

Reviewing the results of my scorekeeping is a little like wandering through a store knowing that there is a security camera trained on you. I felt the eye of Franklin hovering above me, and there seemed to be, though I recognized it was very early, at least a slight change in my conduct. I was conscious of trying to be good. I felt good leaving the house. Kisses all around, a hearty fruit breakfast, and I was skipping out the door.

And it continued at work. My boss and I discussed a trial victory from the morning before, and I can tell that he was impressed with my conduct of that matter and the bail hearings. I should say, at this point, that notwithstanding all the campaign ads that feature alarmingly high conviction rates, the role of a prosecutor in the criminal justice system is not really to win or lose but rather to place all the relevant evidence fairly before the court so that justice might be done. No, I'm serious. They even give us little plaques that say something like that. Thus, I had a nagging sense that my happiness at the victories might, in fact, be transgressions on the virtue chart. Justice, in the Franklin sense, would seem consistent with the quasi-judicial role of a prosecutor. I, on the other hand, was patting myself on the back over a couple of courtroom triumphs. The more I thought about it, the worse I felt.

And then, of course, there is Humility. I was gloating. That seemed to be the direct opposite of Humility. Personal backslapping would certainly merit a tick on the transgression chart. Maybe, I reasoned, I should keep my eye on the ball and concentrate more on Temperance.

As Karma would have it, I paid the price that afternoon. I took a beating in another trial continuation. This one involved a sister stabbing her brother during a drunken argument. Not only did I go down in flames, but an inebriated, homeless woman came into the courtroom during my cross-examination of the accused and began to shout, "She's innocent!" I assumed this was a message from Powerful Goodness. He (or she) was probably still upset about being addressed from the toilet.

I was also a little concerned about my adherence to the schedule part of the program: Ben's day planner. Ben began the day with asking himself what "good" he would do and then ended the day with a self-check on his success. I'd taken a shot at this but it had been halfhearted. On Day 1, I forgot to come up with a "good." On Day 2, I chose "follow up on planning golf trip." While I accomplished that goal, it was hardly altruistic—more self-centered, really. No one is going to bestow on me the Nobel Peace Prize because I successfully planned a trip where I, my dad, a couple of uncles and cousins, and assorted friends beat the bejesus out of a little ball, eat steak, and drink beer. Tomorrow, I resolved, I'd pick something far less self-centered.

I owed it to myself.

On the plus side, I had managed, on Day 2, not to eat any between-meal snacks or anything after supper. This, for a man of my proclivities, was a major victory. It would have been nice to think that I'd mastered this Temperance thing, but I had a feeling that I might not be getting the full flavor of what Temperance means. I was concerned that perhaps I was not committed enough to this first virtue and its real essence. I needed to do more research.

Temperance: The Early Years

As I carried on through my week of Temperance, I was still a little confused about how to follow Ben's virtue. Stuck with it, as I was, I rededicated myself to ferreting out what Ben was after with Temperance. It was more confusing than I had first thought. Perhaps the problem was that despite Ben's admonition to be temperate, he himself was something less (maybe Ben would forgive my snacking after all).

He, of course, acknowledged a level of consistent imperfection early on in his description of the program, but a look at any of his portraits or busts reveals a man given to at least a little intemperance. Willard Randall says that in 1755 Franklin's "face was puffy and smooth from gout, his body overweight and rounded into the peculiar barrel shape of the once-powerful swimmer too long out of the water."[1] That doesn't sound like someone who has completely eschewed eating to dullness. So why put this virtue first, and what did he mean by it? Perhaps the answer is to be found in a little journey into history.

According to an editorial in the *Canadian Medical Association Journal*,[2] a Philadelphia physician named Benjamin Rush, a contemporary of Franklin, penned an article titled "Inquiry into the Effects of Spirituous Liquors on the Human Body and the Mind." Part of the article was a "moral thermometer" that linked drink with points on a scale of intemperance. At the top of his scale, Rush placed water, milk, and molasses, which he associated with health, wealth, and happiness. Wine, port, and beer were farther down, delivering cheerfulness and nourishment "when taken only at meals and in moderate quantity." Spirits and morning drams, at the bottom, delivered "dropsy, epilepsy and apoplexy," leading to "obscenity, fraud and the workhouse or a whipping."

Did Rush influence Franklin, or was it vice versa? Did they compare "moral thermometers"? If they did, I like to think they might have done so over a wee dram, just enough for cheerfulness and not nearly so much that a whipping or the workhouse would follow.

Was Rush the inspiration for Franklin's Temperance, and if so, did that provide any answer to what Franklin meant (and, in turn, what I should have been doing)? Of course, Rush and Franklin must have known each other. Philadelphia was not so big in the late eighteenth century that two learned men would not have encountered each other. Rush's article sold 170,000 copies and is credited with starting the American temperance movement. If Franklin was influenced, what did he take from Rush?

The answer is in the same editorial. Temperance, the editorial declares, is often confused with abstinence. "Abstinence is an extreme and rigid state that sometimes results in prohibition and condemnation; temperance, on the other hand, is a process of self restraint and moderation, the middle road. Plato regarded temperance as one of the cardinal virtues of a society and of an individual."[3]

That helped. I had been wary of the big T because I was thinking of abstinence, which has far too monastic a quality for me. I could live with being temperate, so long as I was not asked to abstain. Besides, who can argue with Ben Franklin and Plato? I resolved to do better.

But then night fell.

Snacks called to me as darkness descended. Like alcohol and smoking and gambling for others, snacking is a rest stop on my personal road to perdition. Not only do I do it with alarming regularity, but I have created new and innovative ways to make foods bad for me. On Night 3, it was one of my favorite fixes for late-night munchies. I took the humble cracker and a block of cheddar—very old cheddar. I cut the strips as thick as a two by four, then arranged the crackers around a plate and lay mounds of these thick slabs of artery-clogging goodness over them so that they became no more than a rumor—a memory under cheese. I then microwaved these bad boys until the cheese had melted enough that it was soft and gooey and the oils had leached onto the plate.

{ *Behold the rain which descends from heaven upon our vineyards; there it enters the roots of the vines, to be changed into wine; a constant proof that God loves us, and loves to see us happy.* }

I was weak. I was intemperate. I was sad. I was full of cheesy cholesterol.

But I would not be defeated in the first week of the virtues. I would carry on, be temperate, and lead a virtuous life (at least for thirteen weeks). Out, out, damn cheddar!

Four Less-Than-Temperate Days Later

Temperance week had come and gone. Had I been temperate? Would Ben be proud?

I had done, at best, okay. No great failures, but no overwhelming success either. I read somewhere that a habit takes about six to twelve weeks to develop, so I suppose I shouldn't have expected the habit of Temperance to be hardwired into my brain just yet. I was only slightly consoled by the fact that my biggest failures during the week were on the other virtues. Given Franklin's formula of concentrating on one virtue at a time, this wasn't a huge concern. I was just being true to the course (that sounds a lot like rationalization, I know).

Had even my mild improvement in Temperance made any difference in my life? Well, I am not sure about it being, as Plato wrote, a cardinal virtue, but I did feel a bit better. Probably psychosomatic.

I certainly think I completed more tasks during the week; thus, I was relatively industrious. I was more aware of Resolution and Justice. Even Order had a greater place in my consciousness. This incremental accumulation of virtue was clearly Franklin's goal. As others have noted, these virtues are not heroic. Indeed, they are a bit pedestrian. No one will become a hero simply by being temperate or moderate. Saints are not borne of Silence or Chastity (okay, maybe they are . . . but not Industry and Order). Yet there is virtue in his virtues. Franklin, seeker of pedestrian virtues in his twenties, became a Founding Father in his seventies.

Yet as I patted myself on my back and started dreaming of Founding Father–type perfection, I began to feel both guilty and inadequate at the same time. I know the source of both feelings. I think it is time for a little confession and personal pep talk, an admission of intemperance at the end of Temperance. Here goes.

I am a felon.

Okay, well, that's overstating it a bit . . . maybe a lot (technically we don't even call felons "felons" where I come from). The truth is that when I was sixteen, I got caught in a bar.

There I was, with several friends, being intemperate in a local pub when in walked several police officers. We tried to escape, only to run headlong into a cop roughly the size of Arkansas. Soon thereafter, my friend and I (along with several other unfortunates) were sent off with a promise of a court date in the near future. I kept the fact of my arrest a secret from my parents.

On the day of my court appearance, dozens of teenagers who had been caught up in the same liquor raid had shown up for court, but apparently none had a surname beginning with A to F. I was the first person called on to plead. As my guilty plea brought the anticipated fine and a stern lecture from the judge, I noticed a man in the front bench of the court house taking notes. This was a concerning development.

After court I approached the note taker and inquired if he was a reporter (the court beat was big in my hometown, there being little other news beyond the 4-H Club and high school hockey scores). When he confirmed that he was indeed a journalist, I asked if he was going to report my name. "What's your name?" he asked. With the foresight of John McCain choosing a running mate, I said, "Cameron Gunn." He smiled, scribbled in his notebook, and said, "I am now."

I thought it best, at this point, to come clean.

It was not a pleasant scene. There was no yelling or screaming. I'm not even sure I got grounded. There were just looks of profound disappointment and ominous promises that the "grandparents" would have to be told. That was worse even than the parental displeasure.

About two weeks after my mea culpa, I was told I was going to help my grandfather (the same one with the cheerful waking ritual) put vinyl siding on a house he was building for my aunt. I had been dreading any contact with my grandparents. The day progressed largely in silence until my grandfather said nonchalantly, "Heard you got in a little trouble."

"I guess so," I replied with trepidation.

"Got caught drinking in a bar?"

"I guess so."

After a little pause and without ceasing his labors, he said, "Well, if that's the worst sin you ever commit, I suspect there's still a place in Heaven for you."

That was it. Nothing else was ever said. Like Bill with Hillary, I was being given a second chance.

I think my grandfather understood that some sins were greater than others and that I had probably beaten myself up enough.

As I reexamined my scorecard for the week, I noticed too many incidents of intemperance. But as my grandfather did, I thought I'd give myself a second chance. My sins were small, and it was early in the game. Perhaps there was still a place in Heaven for me.

TEMPERANCE

EAT NOT TO DULLNESS; DRINK NOT TO ELEVATION.							
	S	M	T	W	Th	F	Sat
Temperance	★★	★	★	★★	★	★	
Silence	★	★			★		
Order		★	★	★			
Resolution	★			★	★		
Frugality			★		★		
Industry					★		
Sincerity							★
Justice							
Moderation						★	
Cleanliness							
Tranquillity	★		★				★
Chastity					★		
Humility		★	★	★	★		

CHAPTER 2

Silence

Speak not but what may benefit others or yourself;
avoid trifling conversation

"YOU HAVE SOMETHING IN YOUR TEETH."

From such sentiments are great romances born . . . or do visits to the dentist begin.

Okay, let me start this story with a little journey into my distant past. After finishing my undergraduate degree, I was making extra money as a bouncer/bartender at a local bar called the Chestnut. It was an interesting place that attracted a mostly blue-collar crowd, with the occasional bikers and, when the live band warranted, university students. On my first shift, after ejecting (gently, or so I had thought) a customer who was clearly unaware of Franklin's virtue of Temperance, I was threatened with a switchblade. That same night, a female ejectee saluted us by hurling her stilettos at us from across the parking lot and pulling a moon.

{ *Silence is not always a Sign of Wisdom, but Babbling is ever a folly.* }

It was the best job I ever had.

The principal benefit of working at a place like the Chestnut was its war zone–like environment. There might have been disease, gunfire, and the constant fear of death, but you formed a real bond with the guy beside you. Friendships, romances, and the occasional business partnership were borne of the shared jeopardy. From my short time at that bar, I met some of my closest friends and, more important, my future wife.

A close friend of Michelle's was one of the prettier bartenders with whom I worked. Notwithstanding a long line of suitors (or perhaps because of it), she decided that instead of bringing a date to a staff party at a local lake, she would bring her friend.

The staff party was one of those "two roads in the wood" moments. I knew that I was interested in Michelle. She was beautiful, and in our one brief, previous conversation (or at least the one brief conversation I could remember), she seemed bright, but that was all I really knew about her. This was a chance to see if an initial flirtation might be worth a greater investment.

I thought it was going well until Michelle said, "Cameron."

"Yes," I replied, more than a little smitten.

"You have something in your teeth."

How does one "more than a little smitten" respond to such a statement? I learned later that she said it because that is her nature. She says what she is thinking. That is who she is. When she doesn't like her food, she sends it back; when the service is bad, she says so. When you have something in your teeth, she says, "You have something in your teeth." (By way of example, when I read her this passage, she said, "I don't remember it the way you tell it, and that's not when I said you had something in your teeth." We've agreed to disagree on this point. Go figure.)

Now I realize that Michelle simply understood the power of

language. She told me that I had something in my teeth because she wanted her potential paramour to get said something out of his teeth. In doing so, she won a husband. I loved her, and love her still, because she uses language purposefully, not maliciously. I loved her because she told me I had something in my teeth. I love her still because I now know that she would never have told someone *else* that I had something in my teeth.

That's the Silence that Franklin wanted. He wanted speech that mattered. He wanted Silence where talking had no purpose. He wanted his acolytes to speak only when it benefited themselves or others.

I was in trouble again.

Remember my self-assessment? I have, in medical terms, a big mouth. I like to talk. I think I inherited it from my mother (okay, I know I did, but my mother is going to read this, and I wanted to ease her into this little confession).

I take little comfort in the fact that I am not alone. North American culture is awash in gossip. There are entire magazines dedicated to news of the dating habits of people famous for being famous. Columns in newspapers are devoted strictly to the foibles and failings of the über-rich. Television shows abound that revolve around tracking the lives of celebrities. It is the modern equivalent of lion feedings at the Colosseum. Think simply of the hullabaloo around Tiger and his dalliances.

Of course, it isn't just the media that gorge themselves on "trifling conversation." Gossip is the vernacular of the modern office; it's what binds people of disparate cultures and races.

Given Franklin's choice for Virtue No. 2, it must have been no different in colonial America. I bet Franklin had a proclivity for it. He was, after all, a journalist. He acknowledged a habitude of "prattling, punning and joking." Ben and I may not share many qualities, but there is common ground here. Trifling conversations are us.

At some point, however, Ben understood that "in conversation it (knowledge) was obtained rather by the use of the ears than of the tongue." So that, at least in the early going, was my goal for this virtue: no gossiping; no prattling, punning, or joking; more listening than talking. Indeed, I decided to speak only well of my fellow travelers. Given that, as a prosecutor, I am paid to describe the nefarious, salacious, and titillating details of people's lives, this had the potential to be a tough week.

I lasted about two hours.

Let There Be Gossip

I barely had time to wipe the sleep from my eyes and address Powerful Goodness before I was slapping the virtue out of Silence.

On Day 1, I rose with the best of intentions. I had firmly set about to avoid all gossip—to speak only when it was a benefit to me or others. I managed to rise, do the Powerful Goodness thing, wish good tidings upon my family, and make it all the way to work without transgression. That, however, was as far as I got.

My undoing was habit. The very power that Franklin sought to harness pulled me into its awful maw and consumed whole my good intentions. So I blame habit . . . and my work colleagues. They are good and decent people (as I hope I am). Until this virtue was thrust upon me, I would not have thought of them as trifling conversationalists. (My boss's nickname among the criminal defense lawyers is the Cobra. He is hardly the sort to prattle or pun.) These are generally serious people engaged in serious work. That is, except for first thing in the morning.

This is where habit creeps in. Each morning is the same. Like salmon swimming back to the river of their birth, we end up in my boss's office to, well, engage in trifling conversation. We discuss the previous night's events, the day ahead of us, and the goings-on in the world. We speak of our own lives and those of others. In short, we gossip. It was into this mix that I took my good intentions and poor record on Silence.

Of course, I wasn't wading into this river without knowledge of the current. I knew what awaited. I had possessed an unfounded optimism that I could resist.

Like a journeyman prizefighter, I was smart in the early rounds. I watched for snippets of gossip among our conversation. When I saw them coming, I sidestepped, backpeddled, bobbed, and weaved. And like that journeyman prizefighter, my early success was my undoing. "This isn't so hard," I thought, and I dropped my guard.

"Oh," I thought to myself as we spoke of someone not present, "that was gossip." Like an old high school classmate passing on a busy sidewalk, I recognized the gossip as it went by, but by the time I was ready to shout it down, it was gone. *Oh well, what's one slip?* Then it happened again—a story about a local lawyer. Damn, I cursed myself for not objecting to the usual backbiting. I needed to up my game. Just as I was thinking of how I would deal with the next incident, one of my coworkers asked me a question about someone, a police officer, and before I could stop myself, I was the gossiper. Metaphorically, I clasped a hand over my mouth. I was no longer just an accomplice; now I was Silence's Enemy No. 1.

I had not even made it through the morning. I started to remember Temperance fondly.

The rest of the day passed uneventfully (relatively), but I knew that if I was to survive the next morning's session, I would need some help. Just saying I wouldn't engage in idle chitchat wasn't enough; I needed to take a more active path. Ben had laid a golden pathway to Silence, but I needed a road map showing how to travel it.

I found some guidance from Lori Palatnik and Bob Burg in their book *Gossip: Ten Pathways to Eliminate It from Your Life and Transform Your Soul.* They describe the Ten Pathways of Positive Speech:

Speak No Evil. Say only positive statements. Let words of kindness be on your tongue.

Hear No Evil. Refuse to listen to gossip, slander and other negative forms of speech.

Don't Rationalize Destructive Speech. Excuses like "But it's true" or "I'm only joking" or "I can tell my spouse anything" just don't cut it.

See No Evil. Judge people favorably, the way you would want them to judge you.

Beware of Speaking Evil Without Saying an Evil Word. Body language and even positive speech can bring tremendous destruction.

Be Humble; Avoid Arrogance. These will be your greatest weapons against destructive speech.

Beware of Repeating Information. Loose lips sink ships. Even positive information needs permission before being repeated.

Honesty Really Is the Best Policy—Most of the Time. Be careful to always tell the truth, unless it will hurt others, break your own privacy, or publicize your accomplishments.

Learn to Say "I'm Sorry." Everyone makes mistakes. If you've spoken badly about someone, clear it up immediately.

{ *He that speaks much, is much mistaken.* }

Forgive. If you have been wronged, let it go.[1]

Oh, gracious. That's quite a list. Body language? Humility? I would even have to say I was sorry? The way this course was going, I thought, I might never say anything else.

Gossip and the Modern Lawyer

In my quest for moral perfection, I had become transparent. Had I been a wiser man, I would have kept my own counsel on the Great Franklin Virtue Hunt. I would have quietly gone about my virtuous business and waited for the results to speak for themselves. However, as disclosed above, I have never let anything speak for itself.

So, as a result of my big mouth, my colleagues were aware of my intention to follow Franklin's virtues. Aware and skeptical. Unmoved by my desire to be better, uninspired by my wish to be virtuous, and unimpressed with my chances of success, they had specifically informed me that they would not be involved in my quest for moral perfection. "Don't drag us into this" had become their collective motto. (Strangely, my wife had given me the same advisory.)

This caused a problem during my quest for Silence. Having dedicated myself not simply to the words of Benjamin Franklin (and my more contemporary guide, Chris Levan) but also to the Ten Pathways of Positive Speech, I had hoped that speaking positively about people would not only make the virtue of Silence more palatable and achievable but also create an environment in which those around me would reflect on the very virtue I sought to achieve. In hindsight, and upon a review of the list, this was more patronizing than humble. That might explain what came next.

As we had done the day before and the day before that and the day before that, we gravitated to our usual prework routine of gossip and occasional griping. This time, however, I was going on the offensive. I monitored the conversation, waiting for an opportunity to knock gossip square in the puss. Opportunity did not take long to knock. A particular name came up, a certain and sure target of negative comment at some point. Seizing the moment, I said something positive about this person. Aha! I congratulated myself. Now I'm rolling. Hopefully the others would follow my virtuous lead.

Rather than the worshipful adulation that I had anticipated, my efforts were met with an incredulous stare, complete silence, and finally the question: "What virtue are you on now?"

This was followed by a discussion, the essence of which was that I was an idiot and that my following a course of virtues was like George W. Bush joining Toastmasters.

At least we weren't talking about someone else.

Resigned to a certain level of indifference from my colleagues, if not outright hostility, I carried on in Silence. Or so I thought.

To understand what happened next, I need to explain that the criminal justice system seems perpetually overburdened to the point of complete collapse. Not long ago, in one North American jurisdiction, the courts were so backlogged that forty thousand cases were dismissed en masse because of breaches of the accused's constitutional right to a trial within a reasonable time. We are a ship that sails along, but we are constantly taking on water.

Plea bargaining is the bucket with which we bale our leaky ship. We haggle, barter, and negotiate. We wheel and deal. We sell off

charges in exchange for pleas, lighter sentences for the certainty of
result. We, both prosecution and defense, become the infomercial
pitchmen of justice.

Why do we do it? It's simple. The system operates on a principle
a little like the old Cold War notion of mutually assured destruction. Both sides have an understanding that if everything went to
trial all the time, the world would end, at least metaphorically.

Ask any criminal lawyer and he'll tell you that plea bargaining
leaves everyone feeling a little dirty. It's not wrong, of course; indeed,
it's judicially sanctioned. Still, there is a certain ickiness to it—like
taking your sibling to the prom. No law against it, but it just feels
wrong. Those of us knee deep in the bilge of the justice system, despite whatever ickiness we feel, are forced to plea-bargain. So when
we do it, we demand a certain amount of trust between counsel—
an understanding that a deal is a deal. When that doesn't happen . . .
well, on that third day of Silence, it didn't.

It was a minor thing really. As part of a plea negotiation (that's
what we're supposed to call them), I had agreed not to submit to the
judge a criminal record that was outdated by twenty years. This is
consistent with the law in my jurisdiction. Such an old record is of
little or no significance to the imposition of a just sentence. It does
not mean, however, that the accused has never been involved in the
criminal justice system, and the quid pro quo in this deal would
include the defense lawyer not suggesting any such thing.

But that's exactly what my opponent said on this particular
occasion.

When it was his turn to address the court, he stood up and said
that his client had never been involved in the criminal process before. This was not part of the deal. Worse, it was an outright lie. The
trust that the process demands was breached.

The immediate problem was easily resolved. I stood up (after taking a deep breath), advised the court of the fact that I had been misled, and made further submissions on the sentence, which the judge promptly accepted. From a virtuous standpoint, however, matters were not so easily resolved. The lawyer involved, sensing that the wisest course of action was a physical retreat, left the building before I could complete my other trials and wrap my chubby fingers around his neck. This left me with an almost overwhelming desire to vent my frustrations to my colleagues—in effect, to bad-mouth my opponent. As soon as the notion of telling others about how angry I was popped into my head, however, I sensed the warning finger of Franklin waving in my face.

Would venting about the other lawyer have benefited myself or others? Initially, I tried to rationalize the situation. If I didn't tell my colleagues, they might be similarly duped by this counsel sometime in the future. Then I remembered that rationalizing gossip was a no-no according to the Ten Pathways. Now my virtuous guides were ganging up on me. Giving in to Silence, I said nothing. Until now, that is.

Ben should have put this virtue last.

Of Peter Lorre and Learning to
Sit Down and Shut Up

There are two truths that all lawyers know: (1) never ask a question to which you don't know the answer; and (2) know when to sit down and shut up. Sort of the bar association's answer to Ben's virtue of Silence.

Easier said than done.

Once, in the not-too-distant past, I prosecuted a trial in which two otherwise upstanding university students were accused of fondling a young woman in a dorm room. It was shaping up to be a typical he said–she said scenario. The victim, a young woman who was still haunted by the betrayal of two men she had considered friends, was a good witness. She told her story clearly and completely without embellishment. It was moving but uncorroborated. Given that I expected both accused to deny her allegations, I was unsure of a conviction. Certainly no one was going to break down and confess on the witness stand to this or any other crime in the real world.

Except that is exactly what happened.

When the first accused took the stand, he did what I had expected: He denied the accusation. The thing was, he seemed very uncomfortable in his denial. As he testified, there was something in his tone, or the cadence of his speech, that seemed wrong to me. I could not put my finger on it immediately, but as he spoke, I knew that something was different here than in almost every other trial I had prosecuted. Finally, it struck me. This young man wanted to be honest. He knew what had happened and he wanted to tell the truth and it was killing him to lie about it. This was very unusual.

I began by having the witness confirm innocuous details, eliciting admissions on things that had little significance. Then I sought some common ground on matters that were not very contentious but that did advance my case. As I wound my intellectual way to the real heart of the story, the allegation of a sexual assault, I ratcheted up the tone of the examination, building it like the crescendo of an opera. Finally, I could sense his defenses weakening, and I put it directly to the accused. Standing just a few feet away from him, I asked in my loudest baritone:

"You've heard what Ms. X. said. She said you fondled her breasts. And she was telling the truth, wasn't she? She was telling the truth, and your denials have been lies?" There was silence for a moment. Even that might have been a victory in any other cross-examination. The accused looked down. He refused to look up at me or anyone else in the courtroom.

Finally, after what seemed like an interminable pause, he lifted his head and, barely above a whisper, replied, "Yes."

So there I was. The one and only witness-stand confession of my entire career, and I didn't know what to do next. A little voice said, "You're brilliant! Now you've got him. Ask him another question. Get him to admit to something else. Make him tell you where Jimmy Hoffa's buried."

Fortunately that voice (which sounded exactly like Peter Lorre) was drowned out by a far louder, less *Casablanca*-like voice that said, "SIT DOWN AND SHUT UP."

"Um, no more questions," I said as I sat down clumsily. I didn't know the significance of it at the time, but I was practicing Ben's virtue of Silence. Anything else I asked was not going to benefit anyone. There was nothing else to say.

I'm not disclosing this because I'm looking for praise or a pat on the back. In fact, the manner in which I asked the question was at least ham-fisted and maybe even legally impermissible. I've disclosed this little snippet because during the week of Silence I got to use the lesson it reinforced.

There were, on that day as on all days, opportunities for the types of conversations that Franklin sought to eschew: a judge with a new car, the absence of a player at noontime basketball (who had been suspended for unsportsmanlike conduct during one of our league basketball games), and various other trifling conversations that were anathema to Franklin's ideals. I avoided these topics as best I could. The real test, however, came when a friend confided her fears about the nature of her daughter's marital relationship.

These, as you may have experienced, are dangerous waters. I never know if someone actually wants advice when they become confessional, or if they are simply looking for validation. I tend to fall in the "If you ask what I think, I'm gonna tell ya" camp. As she spoke, my very core cried out to respond to each of her assertions. In my mind, I said, "You're only saying that because you never went through it," or "Part of the problem is the history between you and her."

{ I resolve to speak ill of no man whatever, not even in a matter of truth; but rather by some means excuse the faults I hear charged upon others, and upon proper occasions speak all the good I know of every body.}

I wanted to tell her to lighten up, to try to see things from her child's point of view. She was coming to me for advice after all (or at least to vent), and it was clear to me that I was just the man to give said advice.

Then a little voice in my head screamed, "SIT DOWN AND SHUT UP!!!!"

Whose voice was it? Franklin, old law professors, my younger self, Peter Lorre? Who knows, but it was firm, resolute, and wise . . . and it demanded Silence. *Speak not but what may benefit others or yourself.* No one was going to benefit from what I was going to say. She didn't really want advice, and more important, I had no legitimate basis for giving it out. I didn't know enough about the situation to make an informed prescription. Two weeks before, these concerns would not have slowed me for a moment. On that day, however, I was living Franklin's virtues. On Day 4 of Silence, a little voice in my head demanded Silence, and I listened. Maybe I wasn't hopeless after all.

Karma and Talking to Computers

I feel sorry for anyone who works at an IT help desk. They are faced with an almost unsolvable problem. On the one hand, average employees want the latest and best technologies. Every advertisement in the newspaper, every television commercial for a computer company, every conversation with the employee's nerdy friends, is a potential headache for an IT department. Butting against this ceaseless demand for new technology is the complete incompetence of the average human over the age of thirty-five to do anything of any value with a computer. "Have you tried turning it off and on?" is now the standard first response to any request for assistance.

And then, of course, there are the viruses, security violations, and unending spam. I hope that they are not specifically targeting me for any particular reason, but not a day goes by that I don't get some sort of penis-lengthening offer. How did this clearly . . . growing . . . industry operate before email?

In response, therefore, to the Gordian knot faced by IT departments across the world, a formidable defense has been developed: inertia.

Requests for the purchase of nonstandard information technology products are generally met with an approval process with the nimbleness of an arthritic octogenarian. No matter the employee's need, no technology is purchased until it is thoroughly studied, examined, and challenged. Generally, by the time any approval is received, the requested software is outdated by two releases. It is an approval quicksand pit.

You might ask what this has to do with Silence. Let me just say that sometimes the virtue gods enjoy a little irony.

Not long before the week of Silence, I had purchased a voice-recognition program for my home computer. I was so impressed with it that I requested that my employer purchase a version for my office. The financial aspect was no problem, but when IT got the request, I hit the wall. Or more to the point, I hit the quicksand pit. On any other day, that might have concluded matters: request, acknowledgment of request, interminable delay, and retirement. This, however, was during the course of my quest for moral perfection. First, I was faced with a natural desire to vent my frustrations. I remembered my virtue, however, and kept silent. (Again, until now.)

More important, however, my Franklinian quest—misguided, unrealistic, and potentially unachievable—must have caught the attention of whatever forces control those aspects of the universe outside the understanding of man (no, it's not bureaucracy). You see, less than an hour after I made the last of what I knew to be my certainly hopeless requests for voice-recognition software, I sat typing a long and laborious legal opinion. Why, oh why, I asked myself, couldn't I be speaking into a microphone and seeing the little words appear on my monitor rather than wearing off the tips of my chubby fingers? As my bruised and battered digits scurried across the keyboard, I lost focus for an instant, hit an unintended sequence of keys, and discovered that my word-processing program was auto-installing something.

I scrambled to stop the auto-install until I read the message. My computer was trying to install the components of a voice-recognition program that had been lying dormant on my hard drive.

In shock, I called the IT department. I told them what had happened, and after a short delay (relative to whom I was speaking); the technician came back and said, "Isn't that funny. The operating system we're running has a voice-recognition program included. We've just never activated it."

I paused and drew a breath. "You're telling me that every employee in this department could be using voice-recognition technology . . . for free?"

"Yup. Looks like it. They'd need a microphone, of course, but once it's activated, it's ready to go."

Let me just step back for a minute and reiterate. On the very day that I had attempted to convince my employer to purchase a program to allow me to dictate into the computer, I discovered, completely by accident and entirely by coincidence, that I already possessed a program that allowed me to dictate into the computer. Now perhaps this, to you reading this removed from the circumstances, may not seem like proof of the existence of some spiritual force dedicated to the proper alignment of the universe. If you are such a skeptic, however, I ask you to reconsider your position. During my week of Silence, I was rewarded for my efforts by being allowed to speak. Perhaps Franklin is in cahoots with my IT department. Maybe I'm just getting punch-drunk from all my virtuous failures.

In any event, all I could manage was "Wow."

There was another pause, then the technician said, "Do me a favor? Don't tell anyone."

"What?"

"Don't tell anyone else about this."

"Why not?"

"Because if you do, everyone will be asking us to activate it. We'll never get anything else done. Just don't say anything, will you?"

Ha! As if. On a day that my Silence had been rewarded, I intended to shout of my reward. And if those to whom I shouted asked how I came to find my treasure, I'd tell them Ben Franklin led me to it.

The Sound of Silence

There is no Silence in my house, not the literal kind at least. I have three children. And a dog. (Actually by the time I was revising this book, we had acquired a second dog. My kids won a bet to force me to get it. That's a story for another book.)

Kelsey, the oldest at thirteen, has, as I have mentioned, special needs. She cannot talk or walk and developmentally she is about one year old. Notwithstanding her lack of speech, she is not silent. She has noises that mean something to her and, after all our time together, something to her mother and me as well. Happy sounds, sad sounds, hungry sounds. We have learned the meaning of the noises she makes, and they can bring joy or pain to our hearts.

Harper, who is seven, is a bright girl. She is empathetic and loving and, like all children, curious. She has questions constantly. I love answering these questions, though Michelle says that I am too verbose in my responses. But I can't help it. I always wanted someone to ask me, "Dad, why is the sky blue?" I hope she never stops asking questions.

Darcy, our baby at five, is . . . well . . . how do I say this knowing someday she might read it? Darcy is loud. She can't help it; she gets it from me. She loves life. She literally loves life, and she shows it by screaming and singing and dancing and laughing. We used to call her the Beast because she ran around the house like a wild animal. She is almost the human embodiment of joy. She is loud.

My home is loud, and I would have it no other way.

Sometimes, however, Silence—real, literal, no noise type of Silence—is a good thing.

Having dedicated myself to the proposition that Franklin's intention in promoting Silence was to avoid gossip, hurtful words, and any speech that was not a benefit, I had ignored the more literal meaning of Silence. Given my natural proclivities (and housemates), the absence of noise is, to me, a mystery of biblical proportions. When my workweek was done, I decided to explore true Silence.

A judge I know books himself into a monastery twice a year. No talking at all—just him and several dozen monks contemplating. That's a lot of Silence. I wasn't sure I could handle that much quiet.

I decided to go ask him about it. When I inquired about the experience, he seemed thrilled that I might follow his example. He told me how the monks and guests eat, work, and pray in silence. Most of your time is spent in your room, he told me, where there is no temptation to speak. It is meant to be a time of reflection.

"Could I bring a book?" I asked.

He seemed a bit taken aback. "You mean other than the Bible?" When I nodded, he continued, his tone less exuberant than it was a moment before. "I suppose. But this is meant to be a place for you to commune with God. The silence allows you to get past the daily concerns that plague us, to clear your mind, to create space for something deeper, something spiritual."

I'm sure he wanted to say, "deeper than *The Da Vinci Code.*" But he was too polite to say something like that.

I was sure I couldn't handle that kind of quiet. If the virtue was to have any real benefit for me, it had to be something easily replicated in my everyday life. I don't often hang out at monasteries (though I once repaired the fire extinguishers at a convent, and all the nuns said to say hello to my dad—that took some explaining to my mom). In the end, I settled on some self-help Silence.

The penultimate day of the week of Silence presented the perfect opportunity to explore real Silence. Left alone at home with Kelsey and Billy, my mentally disturbed beagle, I saw my opportunity. Kelsey was tired, and I knew she would soon fall asleep, and Billy was curled up in a ball on the love seat, dreaming of whatever it is beagles dream of.

And so I sat in Silence.

Or not. I had forgotten the load of dishes in the dishwasher. The *wishhh-whhirrr* sound of detergent being sloshed over our lunch dishes was definitely interrupting my resolute refusal to make a noise. The wash would wait. I turned the machine off and was met with more noise . . . the dishwasher had been masking the sound of the clothes dryer a floor below. A quick trip down the stairs, a turn of a dial, and . . . the sound of our air exchanger. Now I was in trouble. I didn't know how to turn off the air exchanger. Then Kelsey decided to help by making her happy sounds, which were delightful except that they in no way qualified as Silence. It occurred to me, as I listened to this twenty-first-century white noise (and my child), that complete Silence in the modern world is almost unattainable.

Determined to achieve as much Silence as possible, I waited until the air exchanger went silent and Kelsey had fallen asleep. Then I sat and read a book. I immediately discovered another problem in seeking Silence. Silence, the real Silence, must be more than an absence of noise. It is an absence of the things that clutter the mind—the internal noise of modern living.

Life is hectic. The simple clutter of our everyday existence crowds and confuses our waking thoughts. Even the simple, wonderful act of reading fills our heads; this is not Silence. I needed Silence. No reading, I decided.

I laid aside my book, rested comfortably on the couch, and attempted to clear my mind of all conscious thought. Calming myself, I breathed slowly and considered the peace that Silence might bring.

When I woke up, drool drying on my cheek, I was no better acquainted with the peace of Silence. I had discovered, however, the benefit of an unintended afternoon nap.

The Beginning and End of Silence

Why did Franklin place Silence so early in his program? In his autobiography, Franklin wrote:

And my Desire being to gain Knowledge at the same time that I improv'd in Virtue and considering that in Conversation it was obtain'd rather by the use of the Ears than of the Tongue, & therefore wishing to break a Habit I was getting into of Prattling, Punning & Joking, which only made me acceptable to trifling Company, I gave Silence the second Place.

As far as I can tell, no one knows from whence sprung Benjamin Franklin's devotion to Silence. What is certain is that it predated his course of virtue. Indeed, Franklin's earliest writing was done under the pseudonym "Silence DoGood."

Franklin was an apprentice printer to his brother. It was not a happy relationship, if Franklin is to be believed; it consisted of more than the normal servitude such a situation might entail (or at least more than one might have expected in a familial situation). Franklin was desperate to break away from his brother, and he finally achieved this by becoming nominal head of his sibling's paper after his brother's imprisonment for writings embarrassing to the government of the day. The change in ownership was a ruse, but to make it complete, the articles of apprenticeship had to be discarded and secretly rewritten. Ben used the fact that his brother could never speak of the rewritten apprenticeship to escape the situation. A brilliant use of Silence.

How had I done in honoring Franklin's second virtue? Had I succeeded in breaking my own habit of prattling, punning, and joking? Was I acceptable to more than trifling company? I'm not sure that I was ever acceptable to even trifling company, and if I was, I'm not sure that they'd appreciate being called "trifling."

Notwithstanding any failures in the achievement of this virtue, I do now see its benefits. I spoke less and listened more. I avoided gossip and thus learned new things. I held my tongue, and I was allowed to speak. Not bad for Week 2.

I clung to that illusion right up until I looked at the next week's virtue. Order is on deck. I had a house full of knickknacks, a desk full of paper, and a mind full of clutter. I suspected I was about to meet my match.

SILENCE

SPEAK NOT BUT WHAT MAY BENEFIT OTHERS OR YOURSELF; AVOID TRIFLING CONVERSATION.							
	S	M	T	W	Th	F	Sat
Temperance	★	★					
Silence		★	★★★★		★		
Order			★	★			
Resolution		★★		★			
Frugality			★		★		★
Industry	★	★	★				
Sincerity		★					
Justice			★	★			
Moderation	★	★					
Cleanliness		★					
Tranquillity	★	★	★			★	
Chastity							
Humility		★★	★★		★★★		

CHAPTER 3

Order

*Let all your things have their places;
let each part of your business have its time*

MY DOG IS INSANE. WAIT, I DON'T WANT TO OFFEND ANYONE. MY DOG
has canine mental health challenges.

I'm not sure what the *Diagnostic and Statistical Manual of Mental Disorders* diagnosis might be, but whatever is wrong with her tiny beagle brain manifests itself through acute bouts of anxiety. She pees at the sight of bald men (a problem of growing—or receding—proportions in my household), fears all creatures great and small (with the exception of insects, which she hunts with the ferocity of a lion), and once walked backward for two blocks because a frog leapt at her.

Her "issues" would be of little concern if they were not accompanied by

{*A place for everything,
everything in its place.*}

serious physical health problems. Billy (whenever we told someone her name, my youngest daughter, Darcy, used to yell, "She's a girl dog!") has Addison's disease. That was the same condition that caused

President Kennedy such discomfort during his life. And like the American electorate, we didn't find out about her condition until it was too late to make any decisions about our selection. Addison's is an endocrine disorder in which the adrenal gland produces insufficient amounts of steroid hormones. We discovered it when it produced, in Billy, two of its most common symptoms: vomiting and diarrhea. A 3 a.m. cleaning of runny beagle feces from a child's bed is a true test of the strength of the human-pet bond.

I blame Billy, or more precisely our selection of her, on a personal character flaw (my person, not hers): I am perpetually disorganized.

Getting a dog was a natural stage in the evolution of our family. First came courtship, then marriage, next children, and finally, a dog. Michelle and I both had dogs as children. My dog was an overprotective collie named Scottie. Michelle had Chico, a dangerous Dalmatian. So we wanted a dog for our family. A smart, organized, ordered dad would have . . . well, I don't know what he would have done because I am not organized or ordered, and if my selection process for Billy was any indication, I am not smart.

In the dog choice, I dithered and delayed; I procrastinated and postponed. Instead of some systematic assessment of appropriate dog choices—considering their behavior around children, acclimatization to an urban environment, reaction to daytime isolation—I chose another path. I told people we were thinking of getting a dog.

This led to Billy.

Billy came into our life in a manner that has helped me develop a new personal rule: Never conduct business at a funeral.

An elderly relative had passed away, and as often is the case, the funeral service and reception were an opportunity to reacquaint myself with relations with whom I had lost touch. One, a cousin who lived five hours away, said she had heard of our quest for a new dog, was working at a shelter, and had a wonderful dog for us. Had I been more organized, more ordered in my thinking, I would have asked appropriate questions (see above). Instead, all I could think of was, "How much?"

"She's free."

In hindsight, this should have occasioned an amendment to my rule, or perhaps a new rule altogether: Beware of free beagles.

Emails were exchanged. A picture of Billy in repose was our first clue of any problem. "She seems sad," commented my wife.

"And fat," I added. "She's not the best-looking dog I've ever seen."

We decided that physical attractiveness, especially in dogs, wasn't really relevant, and that her sadness, if real, would be dissipated by becoming the newest member of our loving family. One five-hour drive later and we had our new dog.

It would be difficult, in a few short words, to describe the adventures and misadventures of Billy and the Gunns (sounds like a country band), but let me just say that I have learned the following lessons from our time together:

1. The consistency of a dog's stool is a good indication of its health.

2. If a dog vomits or has diarrhea outside the house repeatedly, it will almost certainly vomit or have diarrhea inside the house.

3. Beagles will eat anything, and I mean anything, including things they have already eaten and passed (if that is too disgusting to contemplate, consider it in conjunction with No. 2).

4. Beagles, regardless of their state of health, will run into the woods and engage in No. 3—you just won't know what it is they have eaten until the beagle returns (see No. 2).

5. Doses of dog medication are not to be missed—the results of such neglect will be immediate (see No. 2).

6. Make assessments about how much you are prepared to spend in health-care costs for your beagle before your young children come to love it more than they love you.

7. Once your vet bills pass $5,000, your vet will treat you very much like a part of his family (without giving you a family discount).

8. Never mock pet health insurance.

All that said, Billy has been, on the whole, a great dog. She is patient with the children and loyal to the family. Indeed, she out-ranks me by several notches on the family popularity scale. Her popularity notwithstanding, she has been a learning experience.

Maybe being more organized about getting a dog might not have changed the result. I'll never know for sure because I went about our canine acquisition like I do everything else: stumbling blindly about until something happens, for better or worse.

I have no Order. I am the anti-Descartes. I don't think, but nonetheless I am.

So I was excited and anxious about Order. Temperance and Silence had a whiff of abstraction about them, a sense of the idealistic. Order, though, is pragmatic and practical—a meaty virtue with a chance, in my case, for real-world success.

If only I had better prepared.

Let There Be Order

My initial excitement for Order had been tempered by the stark realization that I am to Order what Tiger Woods is to fidelity. My desk looks like an exploded stationery store. My room (at least my side of it—my wife takes no blame for my disorder) is a World War I trench (absent the rats and cholera outbreaks—most of the time). And my mind is like the London Underground. I am the poster child for nonlinear thinking.

Until the week of Order, I took it as a compliment when I was described as disorganized. But as I stared down at my little chart for the week and thought of the struggle ahead, I was reminded that chaos was not on the list of virtues. Even Ben felt inadequate when it came to Order. He wrote:

> My scheme of ORDER gave me the most trouble; . . .
>
> In truth, I found myself incorrigible with respect to Order; and now I am grown old, and my memory bad, I feel very sensibly the want of it. But, on the whole, tho' I never arrived at the perfection I had been so ambitious of obtaining, but fell far short of it, yet I was, by the endeavour, a better and a happier man than I otherwise should have been if I had not attempted it; as those who aim at perfect writing by imitating the engraved copies, tho' they never reach the wish'd-for excellence of those copies, their hand is mended by the endeavor, and is tolerable while it continues fair and legible.

My heart sank when I read this. If Benjamin Franklin was undone by Order, what was to become of me?

Now, if you knew Chris Levan, my contemporary adviser, you would have undoubtedly told me to take a pass on his advice for this week. If I am a student of impetuousness, he is the master. He has a bit of the whirling dervish about him: a thousand projects going at one time, each in some state of chaos but all coming off in the end despite his lack of organizational skills.

The first time I met Chris, I got some sense of his nature. I was invited to a meeting of a committee at the church I attended. It was my favorite type of committee. We met irregularly, had very little responsibility, and got fed snacks. The purpose of this meeting was to introduce ourselves to the new minister at the church. I anticipated nothing to come of it except for some reasonably good snacking. I was wrong.

Within a few moments, Chris, the new minister, had us all agreeing to take on three new tasks (none of which had the potential for snacking), and he himself had committed to at least five significant endeavors. When he opened his schedule to set up our next meeting, I saw that there wasn't a free hour for the next two months. Indeed, the inside of his day planner looked like it was completed by someone in the throes of a manic episode, with notes and scribbles everywhere. The leftover eraser shreds from numerous deletions and corrections still clung to its pages. It was all more than a little overwhelming.

The thing is that I can't remember what happened to any of those projects and tasks. Maybe they got done, maybe they didn't. What I do remember was that whatever Chris did accomplish, he did through energy and force of will, not organization.

Despite Chris not being an Order guru, he did give me some hope when we discussed this virtue. He told me that Franklin, like John and Charles Wesley of Methodist fame, was living in a social context where abuses of all kinds had shred the fabric of society. Corruption and mismanagement had dealt out destitution and starvation to the masses. Order and control were the only solutions to a decaying political system. So here was a virtue tied up in the very roots of the revolution that was to come. This virtue was very much a product of the circumstances of Franklin's world.

If I was to understand and abide by the virtue of Order, Chris went on to explain, then I needed to seek the right Order for my world, not Franklin's.

Well, that made sense! Though Ben's scheme of virtue was conceived in the early part of the eighteenth century, Ben's musings were cast among the chaos of an imperial power unresponsive to its colonies' and colonists' legitimate concerns and, eventually, a revolution. I, on the other hand, was surrounded by relative peace and tranquillity. But what, then, did Order, in my world, demand of me?

For a lawyer, Order is an imperative that is often ignored. Lawyers need to be prepared and to be organized. But the very nature of the work is dynamic, fluid, and volatile. Order and organization become like Cinderella, the forgotten stepchild waiting for the glass slipper. Prosecutors are the worst offenders against lawyerly Order for three reasons: Prosecutors participate in trials all the time, and thus, through experience (or weariness) they begin to rely on instinct rather than preparation; the volume of cases requires more flexibility of thought than organization of files; and most of the scheduled trials end in a guilty plea at the last minute, and prosecutors come to rely on this outcome (sometimes) to their detriment. Three strikes and you're out at the Order ball game.

On Day 1, I went down swinging.

The whole thing started out rather well. It was a trial of a man accused of defrauding his employer, a political organization, out of a small (in the grand scheme of things) amount of money. The trial was to last the whole day, though I had anticipated being finished in less time. Part of my optimism was based on what I felt were impeccable preparations. I had interviewed the prosecution witnesses on two occasions (a rarity in such a small trial), organized my file completely, and served procedural notices well before the required dates. I was, in the prosecution world, almost overprepared. The Order gods had even taken notice of my efforts. My first witness was an old university professor of mine, indeed one of my favorite professors. My organization and effectiveness would undoubtedly, I reasoned, impress him and show him that I wasn't the dolt that I suspect all my old professors believed me to be.

I called him as my initial witness. His evidence was not that significant. He was there as a setup guy for the big evidence to come later on—a straight man. Notwithstanding that, I had done a run-through of his evidence in my office (twice). Principally he was there to talk about the organizational structure of the association, explain how the office ran, and describe the responsibilities of the accused.

Things went very well—too well (if there were theme music, it would be taking on an ominous tone at this point—imagine the score from *The Omen*). As I concluded my questions, all that remained was to have him identify some checks he had endorsed in blank and that we alleged the accused then took to finance a wardrobe makeover rather than restock the supply closet. The checks themselves were really not in issue, and counsel for the accused had agreed that they be admitted into evidence. More as a final inquisitorial flourish than out of evidentiary necessity, I asked the witness to identify his signature on the checks. Remember the one-question rule from Sincerity? Never ask a question to which you do not know the answer. Remember my inner voice telling me to sit down and shut up? Where was Peter Lorre when I needed him?

I knew things were coming undone when the witness answered, "Yes, on check 412, that is my signature. Yes, on check 413, that is my signature." However, he paused as he examined check 414. A long, uncomfortable pause. It occurred to me as he carefully examined the check that I had never actually asked him to look at them in our preparations. As each second passed, the knot in my stomach tightened.

Finally, the professor looked up and said, "Well, check 414 is signed in my name, but it's not my signature. In fact, there are several checks here that appear to be forgeries."

{ *Employ thy time well, if thou meanest to gain leisure.*}

The defense lawyer was on his feet screaming (okay, talking loudly) about undisclosed evidence (of course, he was afraid I was now alleging that the accused was also a check forger, when in truth I was just ill prepared . . . or stupid . . . or both), the judge was looking completely perplexed (this was not a check-forging trial), and the professor looked anything but impressed. I suspect he was saying, "I always knew this guy was a dolt."

Things eventually worked out. The accused pleaded guilty (months later, after we sorted out the check-forgery issue), the political organization received restitution, and my old professor went on with his life. No long-term harm was done from my failure, but at that moment, standing there with all eyes on me, I was feeling less than Franklin-like.

The virtue of Order had gotten off to a marvelous start.

It Was the Best of Times, It Was the Worst of Times

My struggles with Order are a tale of two women. Like many men, I am torn between my mother and my wife.

I don't know that these two women know they are in competition for my virtuous soul, but their natures pull me in two directions. While they share many common traits, get along very well, and both love and accept me (I hope), they are, in at least one respect, very different. My wife, as you may have gathered, is a pragmatist. She believes in lists and plans and order. She does not like to keep things (other than records), as "things" generally serve no purpose in her mind. She sells keepsakes and discards mementos. She is a creature of practicality, not sentimentality

My mother, on the other hand, is a keeper of things. Her basement is a treasure trove (or minefield if you seek my father's opinion) of kitsch, knickknacks, and life's souvenirs. She preserves her own memories and acquires those of others. She does not believe in throwing anything away because it may have historical value. She does not make lists or have plans—she just does. Though she loves my wife, I have standing orders from her that when she (my mother) passes, Michelle is not allowed to clean out her "things."

So I am torn between these two poles of Order. I see the value of my wife's organization and pragmatism. As a man trained in the law, I know there is benefit in the realism of Michelle's nature. The logician in me likes her approach.

On the other hand, I share, as a product of nature or nurture, my mother's desire to keep the pieces of the past. She is a historian of sorts, and I seem to have inherited that mantel. I eschew lists and plans and seek spontaneity. The romantic in me appreciates her attachment to the preservation of memories.

And thus I tackled Order (still having a limited understanding of the concept) in the context of this struggle (though unknown to the players) for my orderly soul.

The problem was that I was not sure that I could change a lifetime of disorder in the course of a week. Despite my misgivings, I tried. I awoke, again, with good intentions. Hope seemed to spring from my bed with me as I prepared for a new day of Order. But then good intentions met bad habits, or at least disorganized ones. As I have managed to have a pretty good life without Order, I was having a little trouble with self-motivation.

But that was not the quest. No one stands in his stirrups, raises his sword, and calls back to the troops, "To mediocrity!" I was seeking moral perfection here, damn it, and I would not be denied by my own shortcomings (well, actually, that was exactly my expectation, but I was not ready to write things off at that point).

I started off slowly. I cleaned up my office a little, but I think the operative phrase here is "a little." I needed organization on a grander scale. I have attempted organization in the past. I have made checklists and shortcuts for processes at work, but I still seem disorganized. I'd buy one of those "how to get organized" books, but I'm sure I'd lose it.

I needed something grand in vision.

I turned, at least metaphorically, to my wife, keeper of lists and maker of plans. She makes lists for everything: food, recreation, school, housework. Even romance is a matter for a to-do list. I have to tell you, it is a little disconcerting to see something like: "Be nice to Cameron" on a list among: "Buy bell peppers" and "Clean out garbage can."

You can't argue with success, though. If my wife has a list, she is productive—if she doesn't have one, she's a basket case. So maybe on Order, I reasoned, Ben could get an assist from Michelle.

I had a sense, though, that just making a list wasn't going to cut it. Some things don't fit nicely on a list. When does something need a plan rather than a list? Can a task be too big to go onto a notepad on the fridge? Perhaps that was the key to Order: Decide what you want or need to do, figure out how it can get done, break it down

into smaller tasks, and write it down. If I actually did this and achieved any goals, I could get a big star on the virtue of Resolution, which was up next.

So on Day 3 (you might note, if you are following along, that I had done nothing in furtherance of this virtue in two days), my first work task would be to sit down and write out a list of things I needed/wanted to get done, break it down/write it down, and get it done. I felt more organized immediately. Baby steps.

{ Keep thy shop, and thy shop will keep thee. }

Clearly, I was easily impressed with myself.

A Little Satisfaction

Okay, I felt morally good. Not morally perfect. Not even morally great. Just morally middle of the road. But that was a huge step in the right direction. As much as I like myself (and so many people have told me that I like myself that it must be true), I often feel a sense of . . . I don't know how to describe it . . . disappointment. Maybe that's too strong a word, but I know that life is finite, and with every day that passes, goals go unachieved. Every day the world remains unchanged is a day that is wasted—just a little bit.

Isn't that what schemes of self-improvement are all about? Isn't it some kernel (or more) of personal dissatisfaction that drives us to change?

Now don't go jumping down my throat. I am happy. I am very happy. I feel confident. I believe in the potential of mankind (by which I mean man- and womankind, and I believe in gender equality enough to point this out). The problem is, like my beagle at the end of mealtime, I still want more. That's what this book is about, isn't it?

Or is it? I think my uncertainty comes, in part, from my lack of understanding about why Americans seem so fixed on self-improvement. Why do they long to be something different than what they are? Chris has been very helpful on the specific virtues, but I haven't asked him to address the big question.

When you have a big ethical question like that, you find a big ethical guru to help answer it. Like the Pope or the Dalai Lama or Larry King.

While I didn't have access to any of the above, I did have a pretty good resource close to home.

The Very Reverend Dr. Peter Short was the 38th Moderator of the United Church of Canada from 2003 until 2006. The Moderator is the leader of the church, which is the second largest denomination in Canada. The Moderator, according to the church's website, is "expected to give spiritual leadership and public representation" for the church. Peter has written books, was a minister for thirty-one years, and spends his time now speaking and teaching on issues of spirituality across North America. He is a heavyweight on issues of morality and ethics. He agreed to give me a bit of a crash course on why people want to improve.

In his years of ministry and counseling, Peter has seen and counseled untold numbers of people who want to lead a more meaningful life. When I asked him what is the first thing he says to people who ask, "How do I change my life? How do I find more meaning?" his reply was simple. The first thing he tells them is to change the question. *How* is a strategy question: a determination of method. The real question, the one he wants them to ask themselves, is, "Why do I want to change my life?" When you figure that out, the *how* becomes clearer.

So I suppose, in following Franklin, I might have gotten into this thing backward. I was not sure I had any real desire to change at all. I was not even sure I could ask why.

I told Peter that maybe I was looking to Franklin to provide a boost on the ladder of achievement. His response gave me pause. He said, "The world would be a healthier place if there was less ambition."

Okay, so maybe I needed to give more thought to the *why* questions. But for the moment Franklin called. For the moment, the why would have to be simply that I already had one-third of a social experiment finished. The book I had agreed to author on the subject wasn't going to write itself.

Unfortunately, like most of our driven, ambitious, overly committed society, all I had to offer was chaos. Ben, however, wanted Order, so Order it would be.

How was I to create a system to wring Order from my chaos? There is an old saying, "If you want to make God laugh, tell him your plans." I like that sentiment, but I think that it misses an essential characteristic of humanity, part of the reason for our creation. So I would add after those wise words, "If you want to make him cry, tell him you have none." So then as not to make God cry or Ben cringe, here were my plans.

We all (I assume) have dreams, desires, and goals. Remember when you were a kid and adults would ask you what you wanted to be when you grew up? Those early answers were great and dramatic and exciting: astronaut, ballerina, cowboy. No one ever wanted to be an accountant or a mortician. If you are like me, however, the answers, over time, became less grandiose and more realistic (although I looked back at old school materials and found "lawyer" listed as an alternative to astronaut . . . must have been a slow year). Whatever the answer, though, very few of us would have been able to describe a plan to achieve that goal. Yet of all the things in our life, the big goals are the most likely to require some organization and order to come to fruition. No one (other than Homer Simpson and Bugs Bunny) becomes an astronaut by mistake. No one climbs Mount Everest because he or she is staying at a Nepalese Holiday Inn and has a few hours to kill before checkout time.

So for the purpose of my scheme of Order, I decided that the big things should be called Visions. These are the world-changing, earthshaking, fall-to-your-knees types of dreams. As I said, Visions need plans to become reality. So I called the next part of the program Plans. I am nothing if not literal.

Plans are the more concrete version of Visions. If your Vision is to become an astronaut, then the Plan is the answer to the question, "Well, little Cameron, how will you become an astronaut?"

But even Plans need some deconstruction. If your answer to the question above was, "Well, I'm going to become a pilot and go to NASA to become an astronaut," then your Plan to achieve your Vision still needs some specific tasks. Keeping with my literal theme, I called these Tasks. Tasks are those things that are immediate, small things that can be done quickly. These can be part of a larger Plan broken down, or they can simply be part of the detritus of day-to-day living.

So there. If you have a Vision, break it down into Plans, which you then break down into Tasks. Do these, and the next thing you know you're staring out of the front windshield of the space shuttle. I had a plan of Order.

I tried it on Day 4. It worked—sort of. The problem with the scheme was that it seemed too easily defeated by the plans of others. I had my breakdown, all written out into Visions/Plans/Tasks, but just as I would get started on one of *my* Tasks, someone else would ask me to do something for him or her. The needs of others were getting in the way of my wants.

Didn't they know I was trying to be morally perfect? Didn't they understand that I had a scheme of Order to follow?

Of course, that's what life is like, isn't it? Often the plans of others get in the way of our own.

Maybe that was why Ben wanted to achieve the virtue of Order.

Maybe that's why he had to admit that he never did.

A Detour on the Road to Perfection

Ben is a tease.

With my scheme of Order, he had given me just a small taste of what success might await if I follow him, a tempting morsel designed to allure and lure. Then came a significant bump in the road.

My initial success with Order ran headlong into my moral imperfection, manifesting in two aspects of my character: (1) a slavish desire to use technology (boys need toys), and (2) overexuberance.

I should be smarter about technology. Once during an arson prosecution, the projector I was using to show crime scene photographs flashed and then went blank.

Frantically, I got the other prosecutor to ask for a recess, and when the judge and jury went out, I tried in desperation to discover what had gone wrong. I poked at keys and wiggled the mouse. I pulled at cables and prodded at connections. Nothing worked. There was still just a blank screen. The gods of technology were mocking me, I felt sure. As the time neared for court to resume, I stood in the middle of the courtroom and nearly cried. My high-diving act was rapidly approaching a fatal fall.

Then I looked down and noticed that the projector had come unplugged. I will never forget the feeling in the pit of my stomach when that screen went blank.

At least I thought I would never forget it. And yet I forged ahead with my love of technology in trials, with predictable results. In a murder prosecution, we were using a simple program (at least I was learning some lessons) to display photographs. All was working well until, as defense counsel and a police officer sparred over the contents of her notes, my screen saver activated. This particular screen saver was a silly phrase keyed in, as a joke, by a police officer during a previous trial. There were plenty of reasons it managed to come up during an important trial: I hadn't set the timer on the screen saver at a sufficient duration; the police officer operating the computer became distracted by the testimony. It doesn't matter—it just happened. So, as the defense counsel stood beside the witness and in front of an eight-foot-by-eight-foot screen, a message began scrolling in three-foot letters directly behind him:

I'M A SPECIAL DONKEY
I'M A SPECIAL DONKEY

Given my past experiences, you might surmise that I would be cautious and careful in too readily relying on technology.

You'd be wrong (you're wrong about me a lot; I think you overestimate me).

I decided that if my new Vision/Plan/Task program worked, it would work better with the aid of a computer. Perhaps, I reasoned, I could adapt some of the features of my calendar and email program to create an electronic list with reminders and Tasks. Maybe I could create templates and ticklers and all manner of productivity enhancements. I would develop Vision screens and Plan screens and link them to the Task screens preprogrammed into the database. I would be able to track progress and assess my Order skills as I went. As I considered the possibilities, I was almost giddy.

As I sat in front of the computer, no real plan in mind (irony rears its head again), I started playing around with my regular scheduling software. I could easily establish a Task, but I couldn't figure out exactly how I would create grander things like Plans and Visions. I couldn't simply make them a Task; that would have been too basic. I needed higher-level thinking. A little more tinkering produced something that resembled a Plan template. I field-tested it and lost everything I had done. Not to be undone, I tried to reproduce the Plan template and failed. This was going to be more difficult than I had first anticipated.

Finally (and reluctantly) I turned to the Help feature. As I searched around for features of the program, I found a design form and thought I had an "aha" moment. It didn't work. I don't know why; it just didn't.

Okay, I decided, back to the Help feature. I stumbled onto something called InfoPath—another part of the off-the-shelf software about which I had no knowledge. It seemed to hold some promise for creating forms. As I ran through the Help menu and tried to replicate its instructions, I discovered that I had created . . . absolutely nothing. I tried again, and again and again. After several attempts, it occurred to me that the program's designers must have created this as some kind of nerd prank. "Let's put in these instructions for something that doesn't work. Some idiot will putter around until he feels like throwing himself in front of a bus." In disgust, I gave up on InfoPath . . . if that's its real name.

Back to Tasks. Maybe I could simply use the Categories function. That took some jigging. Finally, I managed to get all of the above Tasks turned into parts of Plans (now renamed Categories in the Task feature because I couldn't figure out how to name them anything else). Next I assigned due dates and recurrences where appropriate.

I stood back and examined my creation. It was . . . mundane, hardly the stuff of moral perfection. And it was midnight, so I had wasted almost an entire day.

I could have cursed myself. I could have decried my folly and cast my efforts aside. It seemed as if in seeking Order I had been wasteful of my most precious resource: time. The truth, however, was more nuanced, as it often is. I had, in fact, created a system of organization for myself where none had previously existed.

I am a special donkey. Of course, that might be a step up from sloth. Maybe I was making progress.

It's a Small World

Ben's precept for Order is: "Let all your things have their places; let each part of your business have its time."

I like these precepts. I initially viewed them as outs for Ben, a little moral bet-hedging. But the more I look at them, the more they seem like a real attempt to put flesh on the bones of the virtues. Franklin knew that a virtue like Order meant more than being organized in your business. He wanted (at least I hope he did) life balance, though he would never have named it thus. He knew that a person would not be successful in life until all the parts of his or her life received attention.

But if he knew this, he wasn't particularly good at it. He was a man of accomplishment. He invented, he worked, he led. He was an adventurer and a traveler. Ambassador, politician, author—he was one of history's most accomplished men.

And yet, in one respect—his relationship with his family—he seems to have been . . . imperfect. He had an illegitimate son, William, whom he raised without apparent concern for his status or how it might be viewed. Indeed, he used his influence and wealth to make his son a powerful figure in colonial America. The Revolu-

tion, however, came between them when William chose the Royal-
ist side. Franklin eventually cut off all ties with him. They never
really reconciled, despite William's attempts to do so.

Franklin's wife also fell victim to his ambitions. As he became
more important and successful, he spent more and more time away
from home. As the relationship between England and her colonies
deteriorated, Franklin was dispatched to England to make the case
for several of the colonies directly to the British. He ended up
spending years away from his wife, Deborah. Eventually she fell ill
and died while her husband politicked across the ocean.

Some of Franklin's critics have used his family relationships to
malign his character, but I think it points only to his humanity. He
was, as we all are, morally flawed, and I think he recognized this,
both when he created his course of virtues and when he wrote about
it later in his autobiography. And when he calls for attention to all
parts of one's life, it seems to me that it is said with a note of sadness, a point of regret he would have wanted to spare others. And
so I decided to dedicate the last day of Order to my family.

Mindful of the project in which I was engaged, I didn't want to
entirely abandon the program of virtue. As I examined my course
of Order, it was apparent that it was weighted heavily on personal
and work achievements and largely ignored the most important
aspect of my life, my family. My wife and I often speak of our
dreams for the future but wonder why so many plans seem to pass
by unaccomplished. Such is the nature of life for parents of young
children—too busy living to plan. I think that there is something
good in simply living life, but perhaps by doing so we miss an opportunity. As part of my virtue-seeking program, I decided that on
the weekend of Order, as I communed with my family, I would
actually impose some Order on my home life. My Vision/Plan/Task
scheme would get field-tested, Gunn style.

The first step, I decided, was to sit down with my five- and seven-year-old daughters and ask them what it was that they wanted out of life. As I asked the question, it occurred to me that I was an idiot. Who asks a five- and a seven-year-old what they want out of life? They're five and seven! They want whatever makes them feel good in the moment. Despite being relatively intelligent girls, they have no concept of big and small in the metaphysical sense (nor should they be asked to make the distinction). They are creatures of the concrete, not the abstract. They are five and seven. All they wanted out of life was another cookie.

But I was not to be deterred. I would have Order—a plan for my home life. I would create Visions. I would break those down into Plans. These Plans would become Tasks. We would have Order in this family, Order in the best traditions of Benjamin Franklin.

In the end what I got was a nascent plan to take a trip to Disney World. Hardly grand Vision stuff, but by the end of the morning, we were checking out the Disney website and guessing which rides we'd like the most. We assigned a date to the trip, put it on the calendar, and took the first tentative steps toward planning a family vacation. We were having fun in a very middle-class, bourgeois sort of way—hardly virtuous. Oh well, Mickey, here we come. Ben would have to wait. I bet he would have liked Space Mountain.

ORDER

LET ALL YOUR THINGS HAVE THEIR PLACES; LET EACH PART
OF YOUR BUSINESS HAVE ITS TIME.

	S	M	T	W	Th	F	Sat
Temperance		★			★	★	★
Silence		★		★		★	
Order		★	★★	★		★	★
Resolution		★★	★	★			
Frugality		★	★		★	★	
Industry		★		★			★
Sincerity							
Justice							
Moderation							
Cleanliness		★		★			★
Tranquillity		★				★	
Chastity							
Humility		★		★		★	★★

{CHAPTER 4}

Resolution

Resolve to perform what you ought;
perform without fail what you resolve

AT THE RISK OF HAVING SOMEONE FROM THE TELEVISION SHOW *INTER-*
vention turn up at my door, I have yet another confession. By my
senior year in college, my mother believed I drank too much (she
may have developed the belief long before that, but she kept it to
herself up to that point). I don't want this to sound overdramatic.
She didn't drag me to an AA meeting or
kidnap me and have me deprogrammed. *{ Tomorrow, every Fault*
She was simply concerned that, having *is to be amended; but*
invested heavily in my postsecondary *that Tomorrow never*
education, I was spending too much of *comes.}*
my time in the campus bar.

My mother is a clever creature. She knew that interminable parental lectures have little effect on inveterate behavior. Better the
carrot than the stick, especially with men/boys barely out of their

teens. So she waited, picked her shot, and when I came looking for a favor, she went all Don Corleone on me.

At Christmas of my senior year, my roommates had signed up for a spring break bus trip to Florida. After nearly begging my parents to send me as a graduation present, my mother surprised me. Notwithstanding the burden it would place on their own finances, they quickly agreed to the trip. "There's a catch," said my mother. "We'll send you if you agree not to touch a drop of alcohol from Christmas to spring break."

If ever there was a time for Resolution, this was it.

So I took up the challenge (a little chagrined that it was proposed at all) and steadfastly refused to imbibe for a solid three months. I was on the honor system. My university was only two hours from my hometown, but there would be no motherly monitoring, no daily checkups. If I was to keep up my end of the bargain, it was all on me. In the end, in the conflict between youthful intemperance and honor-driven resolution, it was no contest.

For three months I didn't hold, smell, drink, or even clean up alcohol. I became the world's most dependable designated driver.

Finally, the three months came to an end, and I duly reported to my mother (who had already paid for my spring break trip) that I had maintained my end of the deal. I had been resolute; I had, in the words of Franklin, "performed without fail what I resolved." And never had there been a more concrete reward for resolution: I was on my way to Florida. I, several of my closest friends, and eighty other students gathered at the front doors of the Student Union Building to board two buses bound for sunshine, girls in bikinis, and—my deal being over—beer.

In fact, the deal having been completed, the beer started to flow even before the bus arrived. I joined my friends, and the other bus trippers, in toasting our voyage. We continued to toast as the bus left the university. The consumption continued following a trip to the duty-free shop at the border and kept right on after a stop at the world's cheapest liquor store (or so it seemed to us) in tax-free New Hampshire. It flowed and flowed and flowed.

And then the bathroom on our bus broke.

Short of actual physical violence or serious illness, there can be little to compare in discomfort to a bus full of . . . well . . . full bladders, a driver on a schedule, and an interstate short on rest stops.

Things looked to be coming to a head (so to speak) when I decided that the driver must stop. Deputized by my fellow travelers, I spoke to our bus driver and asked politely if he could stop. "Nope. My instructions are to get to Florida as fast as I can. No stops until we get to the next rendezvous point."

I explained our dire circumstances. No luck. I appealed to his conscience. He had none. I begged for a little understanding. He ignored me. It was only when I threatened—Mom, don't read this—to use his head as a urinal that he came to a screeching halt at the next rest stop.

It was as if someone had opened the doors to a stockade. Drunken college students poured from the doors of the bus like runners before the bulls of Pamplona. I was struck, after my own relief was found, with the folly of three months of clear-headed resolution wasted in so stark and crass a fashion.

So I know the need for Resolution. And I know that even the mastery of it can be undone all too easily.

And never has there been a more timely resolution than Resolution. Like a white knight charging forth at the climactic moment in a battle, Franklin's admonition to do what I ought came just at the moment in his course of virtues that I was failing (or at least faltering). Sure, I was still following the virtues, tracking my successes and failures, and generally heeding the words of Mr. Franklin, but my heart just wasn't in it. My ethical mentor, Chris, had taken the week before Order off, and when he returned, I took up the course again. Unfortunately, even a one-week interruption in the process of a course of virtue seems to take some of the steam out of virtuousness. To add to my dilemma, I had already done much of the work for Order; thus, the week was easier than it should have been. The end result of all this was that I was being less than virtuous. And then along came Resolution.

But like my bus trip failure, I simply needed some relief and a second chance. What has been undone can be done again.

Chris's guidance to me was generally in the form of written interpretations of Franklin's, but occasionally we would meet over a glass of wine at a local café. At one of these, he told me that Resolution was all about second chances. Resolution, Chris explained, is about the belief in imagination, hoping, laughing, and loving. These things sound really good over a glass of red wine.

And so I resolved to set forth with renewed vigor. A second chance was all I needed (okay, technically a fifth, a sixth, maybe an eighth chance—the number is not important).

I was feeling good.

I'm sure you can imagine where all this was headed.

Undone by Email

Email.

The very word makes me shudder. If there is any single villain in my efforts to follow Franklin, it is email. If Resolution is Superman, emails are Kryptonite. Pervasive, invasive, insidious.

What did we do before email? It seems that 50 percent of my day is spent reading, responding, considering, or ignoring emails.

And now, with the advent of web-enabled smartphones, they stalk us like emotionally disturbed exes. There should be someone you can call to get a restraining order against emails.

I find that emails have also engendered in me an irrational dislike of those who seem incapable of surviving without instant access to an email server. On buses, in coffee shops, at malls, in meetings, and at dinner and over drinks, there is always someone pulling out a BlackBerry or a PDA and checking to see what issue of global importance has just deposited itself in his or her in-box (it's amazing how in one generation the word "in-box" has acquired an entirely new meaning). As I watch them tap away with their little calloused thumbs, I feel like wrenching the device from their hands, flinging it as far as I can, and screaming, "You're not that important. You can wait until you've finished your soup before you see what other fool is rudely sending off generally trivial information."

I know, that doesn't seem very virtuous, but stick with me. Maybe Tranquillity is going to be a welcome week.

And yet, as much as I hate emails, I'm not sure how I would survive without them. Perhaps my annoyance for those that draw their PDAs like weapons is that I see myself in them. Their weakness is my weakness; their addiction is my addiction. And so it was on Day 1 of Resolution. Blue tights and flowing cape gave way to bits, bytes, and a glowing monitor. The story really starts with an overweight politician with oversized ambition.

On the weekend that Order ended, and before Resolution began, a politician (from my hometown, no less) quit the caucus of the governing party in protest. (Okay, time for another dose of Canadian electoral education. Canada is a parliamentary democracy, as are its provinces. Governments hold power when they have the majority of seats in their respective legislative assembly. Thus, when someone quits the caucus—leaves the government—it's a big deal. It's a bigger deal if you're clinging to power with a margin thinner than butterfly wings, as was the party in question.) The reasons for the rift were unclear. The politician claimed it was a principled stand. He had been passed over for an important position and insisted that his constituency deserved representation at the seat of power. His departure was a blow to a party holding a slim majority.

The party's leader alleged far less scrupulous motives for the departure. He suggested that the departure was the last act of a blackmailer who had sought a job (for a friend), a position of power (for himself), and a judicial appointment (for an adviser).

The politician loudly denied the allegations of his former leader and took up his place as an Independent. The drama was made all the more spectacular by the shoot-from-the-hip style of the politician in question. It was the talk of the town by Monday morning (and coincidentally Day 1 of Resolution).

So there I was, reining in my gossip tendencies with as much virtuous strength as I could muster, when I read a newspaper column on the scandal by a former politician. It was well written, engaging, entertaining, but, in my opinion, completely and utterly wrong on the virtues of the parties involved. This would have been of no import except that this columnist happened to be my cousin.

I am fortunate in my family, and to say that I am close to my cousins would be an understatement. Since I am an only child, they serve as my brothers and sisters. I have cherished, and still cherish, that strong familial bond. Indeed, as we have grown from children playing in my grandparents' yard to adults spread across the vast expanse of North America, we have remained not simply relatives but friends. We attempt to keep in contact, to spend time together, and to support one another.

In the case of this particular cousin, the former politician, we talk on a regular basis, used to try to have coffee at least once a week (before he moved for work), and entertain each other with our views on politics and the world. Our views on this scandal were, as I've said, in diametric opposition. The disagreement (friendly to be sure) was too entertaining an opportunity to pass up.

I dashed off a quick email assailing his take on the scandal, and congratulated myself on my wit and intelligence. I ignored how many of the virtues I had trammeled in both my email and my self-congratulations.

Shortly after sending off my missive, I received a reply. It was sarcastic, challenging, opinionated, and unrestrained. It was also very funny. It could not go unanswered.

I reaffirmed my earlier points on the merits of the two principles (indeed, my general take on the issue was that neither side had any merit, there were no "Mr. Smith Goes to Washington" types among the players, it smacked of political opportunism, and it called for, in the words of the Bard, a plague on both their houses). Satisfied that my argument was unassailable, I hit send. Almost before I could turn in my chair, a tinny chime announced a new message. This was war.

As the day passed, I cursed not the distraction of the emails but the business of my day that in turn distracted me from my electronic debate. Indeed, notwithstanding my Resolution to be resolute, by the end of the day I had spent at least two hours of my work time composing and responding to emails with my cousin. The repartee was witty, the writing entertaining, and the dialogue stimulating; it was not, however, something I get paid to do, and certainly not something that had been on my to-do list.

I had, over the course of the afternoon, run roughshod over Franklin and his virtues. I had gossiped, I was anything but industrious, I was immoderate in my views and unjust in my comments,

and I had not been silent. Sincerity surrendered to humor in my
email exchange; Humility was nowhere to be found; and, above all,
I had not resolved to perform what I ought, nor had I performed
without fail what I had resolved. If I had been drunk, been un-
washed, and bought something I didn't
{ *Energy and persistence*   need, I would have bowled a perfect
conquer all things.}   anti-Franklin game.

It is too easy to blame the whole
episode on the ease of email. My failure was more elemental. Despite my best efforts to be resolute, I had been the opposite. As I
contemplated my debacle, a colleague came into my office and
commented, with some amazement, on the level of organization I
had achieved. "Wow, you must really be getting some things done,"
she said.

I thought of Chris and said to myself, "I believe in third
chances."

No . . . Well, Maybe

Part of my problem in keeping my Resolutions is what my mother
described in her initial assessment of me: an inability to say no. I
don't know why I can't say it. I just know that the problem manifests itself, as it always does, in my taking on too much. In the last
few weeks I have agreed to lecture to a criminology class at one of
the local universities (for free), teach a course on the justice system
to a group of private-investigation students (for free), and establish
a charity to facilitate pro bono work by local lawyers (obviously for
free).

Given my need to focus on Franklin, this little personality flaw
is becoming a problem. It seems just as I begin to master one of the

virtues, a transgression of another occurs. Like holes in the dike, I stretch to plug one as another stream of vice-filled sludge spews forth. There seems to be no end to the things that I should resolve to do. Perhaps that's a good thing; Franklin has made me conscious of my deeds and actions. On the other hand, I may be suffering from a significant bout of overcommitment.

I have also noted a particular pattern in my vice-like behavior. It seems the further I progress past a particular virtue—Temperance, for instance—the less likely I am to follow it. For instance, once my family had gone to bed last night, I opened up a package of Hershey's Kisses, nibbled away, and then went to some pains to hide the evidence of my action. This was not a one-time occurrence. Cheese and crackers, salami, chips, and chocolate have all been the source of my undoing over the past two weeks.

So why do I stretch myself too thin; why can't I say no? I expect it may be some innate need to be liked, some fear of rejection born of low self-esteem. It doesn't matter. This book isn't about following Sigmund Freud; it's about following Benjamin Franklin. And Franklin won't put up with obstacles to moral perfection.

Perhaps, then, one of my resolutions should be to do less. Now that may be antithetical to the very notion of this book, but there is something to be said for focus. Franklin wasn't suggesting that we needed to resolve to do everything but rather that we resolve to do what "we ought." Maybe what I ought, in this case, is to do less and be better at it. Maybe if I finally learned to say no, I would have an easier time achieving yes. Geez, that's almost profound.

I have known the freedom of no once before. Overcommitted, overworked, overtired, and overexposed, I decided that I needed to scale back. One by one, as fiscal years ended, I shed volunteer and nonessential work-related committees, paring them down to . . .

none. As people called to seek confirmation that I would continue to serve at the end of a yearly mandate, I politely declined. When asked the reason, I was honest. It was surprising how understanding people were. My fears of disapproval or a lack of approbation were unfounded. As more and more of my responsibilities evaporated, I felt free. A burden, albeit an important one, had been cast off. I was unencumbered (except for all my nonvolunteer responsibilities). It was a good feeling.

It didn't last. Once the initial euphoric sense of freedom diminished, it was replaced by some sense of longing with a healthy dollop of guilt. There was a reason, I came to understand, that I had volunteered in the first place. There was a purpose for my commitments; there was a goal with my burden. So, slowly, with a self-made promise not to take on too much, I began to reacquire volunteer commitments. A committee here, a sports team there. It felt good to give back again.

THEN ONE DAY I LOOKED UP AND I WAS HELPING COACH TWO SOCCER teams (a sport I know almost nothing about), sitting on the board of several community foundations, and representing my company on no less than eight work-related national committees. I was right back where I had started.

{ Does thou love life? Then do not squander time; for that's the stuff life is made of.}

So the lesson, I'm sure, is this: Resolve to say no—no to being overburdened, no to being overcommitted, no to the things that take you away from what is important. Then resolve to say yes. Say yes to those things that are important and only those things.

So here I go; I resolve to say no to being overburdened. The next person who asks me to contribute to a worthy project is going to get a resounding NO . . . well, maybe.

A Tale of Castration and Second Chances

There ought to be some sort of rule against engaging in nostalgia-inducing activities while conducting life-altering programs of virtue. No good can come from long plaintive looks at life's journey past while one is so intensely contemplating the future.

At the request of one of my colleagues, who supplements his inadequate prosecutor salary as a part-time lecturer at one of the local universities, I agreed to speak to his fourth-year criminology class on the law of search and seizure. Doing the lecture was no great difficulty; I often lecture to law students, police, lawyers, and even judges on the topic. Going to the actual class was, however, more than a little traumatic.

Looking out at the bored, slack-jawed students near the end of term, indeed likely near the end of their college lives, I was struck by the notion that their futures were like a great unmapped expedition—unknown, yet full of promise. I hated them.

Not so long ago, I, too, was a slightly bored student facing the end of my university career. In fact, if I had liberally applied Grecian formula (to the spots where there is still hair) and sucked in my gut, I could have been one of them. That's not the real problem, of course. The real problem is that these students reminded me of why I was doing what I was doing, why I was following Franklin. I was doing it because I am a failure.

Perhaps you feel I am being too hard on myself. Cut it however you want, there is no disputing that I have done less, given less, achieved less, earned less . . . *am* less than I could have been when

I sat in the same seats that those students did. As I looked out at them, trying as they were to stay interested in my talk, I could barely restrain myself from rushing down from the podium, grabbing them by the shoulders, shaking them violently, and screaming, "Live every day!"

For a moment I flashed back to a motivational speaker who visited my high school when I was in the twelfth grade. You know the type. A self-promoting, supercheerful, somewhat humorous professional speaker dedicated to motivating the graduating students by some variation on the theme "these are the best years of your life." That message was always quickly followed by "you have the whole world in front of you." Maybe I was jaded, but even as an eighteen-year-old, I thought it seemed slightly incongruous (and less than motivational) that I was being told that my whole life stretched in front of me but that the best of it had already passed. Maybe that's why I wanted to slap some enthusiasm into my temporary students (metaphorically speaking, of course).

I should have told them about Héloïse and Abelard. Theirs is a tale of second chances.

According to Chris, Abelard was a renowned scholar in medieval France and Héloïse one of his most brilliant students. In an age when women were treated as little more than slaves to their husbands, Héloïse was learned, spoke several languages, and was recognized as an intellectual giant. It didn't go unnoticed that she was also a hottie. Abelard fell madly in love with her, seduced her, and got her pregnant. Then, for his transgressions, he was castrated by her uncle.

Really. They castrated him.

Bet you didn't see that coming. Not with all that talk of second chances.

Héloïse, getting in my mind the better part of the deal, went to

Britain to give birth out of the limelight, and Abelard fled into the wilderness. That could have been it: one baby, one woman shamed, and one eunuch. But it wasn't. That was actually the beginning of their romance.

Years pass . . . the two lovers were separated by geography and obscurity . . . not to mention the castration. Eventually they began a correspondence, until Abelard got himself into trouble with the Vatican, was threatened with excommunication, and fell ill. Héloïse heard of his dilemma and had her now dying lover brought to her priory, where she nursed him. After all the road blocks and obstacles, two people who had run out of second chances got a final second chance to be together. Abelard died soon after and was buried in the graveyard of the nunnery so that Héloïse could be close to him, and when she died, she was buried with him . . . two coffins, one grave.

That was what I wanted to tell the students—okay, not this specific story. I'm not sure how they would have taken a story about a teacher seducing his student and then getting castrated. What I wanted to tell them was that there are no second chances and yet there are always second chances. "Calling all slugs and sloths! Time to get off the couch of self-induced complacency." Television instills in us a spectator mentality. We watch our lives from the stands. We live and love vicariously through the stories of others. And to those of us who are caught in this kind of life-by-proxy, Ben Franklin strengthens our resolve. "You are more than a lifeless lump. Don't do it. Don't put off until tomorrow what you ought to resolve for today."

If I can do it, a self-professed failure, then they could do it, before their failures were upon them. If Abelard could do it, minus his . . . well, you know . . . anyone can do it. That's what I ought to have told them. Unfortunately, all I did was bore them with details of the law of search and seizure. Although they did perk up at the mention of strip searches.

Maybe I'll get a second chance next year.

My brief return to the halls of academia had put me in an introspective mood. Why is it, I asked myself, that I should want to change my behavior? Notwithstanding my self-effacing barbs about my admitted failures, I like myself. I like the choices I've made. I like the person I've become, I like my family, I like my job, I like my life. Why had I taken up this challenge to follow somebody else's suggestions on what constitutes virtue?

Maybe the answer was wrapped up in the very reason that I wanted to give a metaphorical kick in the ass to my slump-seated criminology students. My journey to virtue is more about embracing every day as an opportunity for improvement rather than wholesale change.

I remembered an article I had read and saved from the American Psychological Association online magazine. It was called "Solutions to Resolution Dilution"[1] and was written by author Sadie F. Dingfelder (I love that name). The article detailed some chilling realities for anyone seeking to be resolute: After two years, only 19 percent of resolvers still stuck to their resolutions.

The author found that a predictor of success was self-efficacy, or the belief that one can effect and maintain change. Certainly Ben was the ultimate believer in self-efficacy.

Right. Time for a little affirmation. Say this along with me if you're following this program (if you're not, this would be a good time for a snack break—please get me a hunk of cheese and some crackers while you're up). "I am not a failure. My moments of weakness are not full-on relapses. I resolve to carry on. I resolve to be better. I resolve to be more virtuous." Are the cheese and crackers here yet?

Lessons in Resolution and Humility

As the week of Resolution wound its way to its inevitable conclusion (a lack of success, a feeling of shame, and a commitment to do better), I was struck with the notion that I should at least be learning lessons from my failures.

What, then, were the lessons of Resolution?

Lesson No. 1: Beware the enemies of Resolution (even the unwitting ones). This virtue has enemies and challengers that lurk around us everywhere. Take my cousin. He is an honorable, intelligent, erudite man, and I find discussions with him intellectually stimulating. Unfortunately, faced with the chance to discuss an ongoing political scandal with him, I failed to be resolute. I gave in to temptation and I stopped doing what I ought.

Lesson No. 2: Learn to say no. If we allow ourselves to be overwhelmed with activities and projects, nothing will be achieved.

Lesson No. 3: Acknowledge transgressions, fix the problem, and move on. This lesson is a hybrid. It is human nature to want to achieve; it is just that we don't understand our natures very well until we see time passing us by. It is important to understand that life is finite, that there are no do-overs, and that carpe diem has nothing to do with fish. On the other hand, don't become wrapped up in achievement. Enjoy life. Be resolute in doing so. And above all else, don't give up. Little failures are not "full-on relapses."

Lesson No. 4: Finally, pay attention to the small things. I like the big picture, but if we don't pay some attention to detail, there will be no big picture. You might, at this point, be flipping through the preceding pages wondering where that little nugget of wisdom arose. Stop flipping; you won't find it above. Look below.

If you looked at my weekly chart of transgressions and thought that I had been particularly virtuous, you would have been wrong. At the end of the week of Resolution, so wrapped up was I in being resolute that I failed to do what I had resolved. I had not filled in my weekly chart since the first day. Not a mark. That was an embarrassing lesson in Resolution. I just wasn't sure where to note the transgression.

RESOLUTION

RESOLVE TO PERFORM WHAT YOU OUGHT; PERFORM WITHOUT FAIL WHAT YOU RESOLVE.							
	S	M	T	W	Th	F	Sat
Temperance							
Silence		★					
Order							
Resolution		★					
Frugality							
Industry							
Sincerity							
Justice							
Moderation							
Cleanliness		★					
Tranquillity							
Chastity							
Humility		★					

CHAPTER 5

Frugality

*Make no expense but to do good to others or yourself,
i.e., waste nothing*

I IMAGINED GETTING MARRIED BEFORE I HAD EVEN GRADUATED FROM
high school. Unlike all those commitment-phobic men that seem
to populate every sitcom and date movie, I looked forward to the
day when I would be tied by the bonds of marriage to one person,
for better or worse, for richer or poorer,
till death do us part. More than that, I
imagined I would be the perfect husband. I am, or at least I was, a roman-
tic. I believed that once I had found the woman who was perfect for
me, I would never take her for granted. I would never forget to tell
her that I loved her. I would never give her reason to ask, "Why did
I marry *this* guy?"

{*A penny saved is a
penny earned.*}

But that's not the way marriage works. It is not the stuff of fairy
tales and imagination. It is, like the rest of life, something of a
struggle. Children, jobs, houses, housekeeping, mortgages, credit

cards—all of it. These are the killers of romance, the assassins of *amore*. When marriages work well, they are part of the shared joy and journey, in some cases—as with children—the best part. But they don't make it easy to be Prince Charming.

And if there is an evil stepmother in this already jaded fairy tale, it is money. Study after study has pointed to money as the principal area of conflict for couples. It is little wonder in our credit-heavy, beat-the-Joneses, consumer consumption society that money problems would be number one. Arguing with my wife over our finances was not part of that romantic, stress-free, wedded bliss that I imagined. But neither was my gaining fifty pounds and losing most of my hair (Michelle probably hadn't anticipated that part either).

We don't know what we're getting when we marry someone. The choice of a mate is a big sloppy soup of emotions and genetics and pheromones. I suspect that some people wake up and discover that they won the spouse lottery. Others feel like Ling Ling the panda: captive and expected to reproduce.

The majority fall somewhere in between. If we're lucky, our expectations and reality aren't that far apart. When my wife married me, I'm not sure what she thought she was getting, but I suppose she hoped that she was getting someone who could at least bear his share of the financial load. Once again, I've been a disappointment.

It's not that I don't earn a reasonable income. I do okay. It is simply this: Whenever money comes within twenty feet of me, it is instantaneously repelled by some mystic force. Like two similarly charged magnets, my pocket pushes away money at a speed that my online banking system can barely track.

Anyone who has viewed my wardrobe, looked at my vehicle, or taken a mental assessment of the consumer items around me would be surprised to learn that I am not frugal. It is apparent that I spend very little money on myself—at least on things that are tangible. In fact, if you asked me where my money goes, beyond some mutterings about how expensive children are or about being mortgage poor, I really couldn't identify how it is that I've managed to accumulate a smaller savings account than an eight-year-old paper boy. All I know is that despite my reasonable income, my lack of expensive tastes, and a wife who is diligent about tracking our household expenses, I epitomize the phrase "paycheck to paycheck."

Michelle, in her desperation to explain the situation into which I have immersed her, will tell you that she was very good with money before we met. Working two jobs while going to college, she managed to save a substantial amount of money. Then I came along, and whatever magic she had with currency disappeared. Now she struggles mightily, aided only by the Internet and a dubious receipt tracking system. Michelle does battle against my innate ability to dwindle away our finances with no apparent vices—at least not expensive ones.

I'd like to offer her some explanation, but as I said above, I am at a loss. On days of particularly low self-esteem, I simply say that I am bad with money. More charitable days bring the logically flawed justification that my inability to accumulate wealth is something of a positive trait. I am unconcerned, I rationalize, with money. Money is a base, demeaning method of exchange and nothing more. Gold (or more precisely the want of it), as we all know, is the root of all evil. We are awash in a sea of consumerism, I trumpet from my soapbox, and I want no part of it. I am not motivated by money, nor am I for sale.

Oh, if only that were the real reason.

I truly am not motivated by money, not in any significant way at least. I often speak and give lectures to groups and am sometimes offered compensation. "No, no," I say with all the self-congratulation

I can muster, "I cannot accept any remuneration for a task that I feel is part of my ethical responsibilities." Michelle never gets that one.

Yet, on the other hand, I am as guilty of consumerism as any of my neighbors. I like gadgets, salivating over any new technology, and when I close my eyes and dream of a perfect life, it almost always includes a foreign-built convertible and an in-ground pool. So any principled opposition to the accumulation of wealth is an ex post facto justification. It is not the reason I can't balance my checkbook (actually, I have no idea where our checkbook is).

So from whence does this particular character flaw arise? I can't blame my parents. They managed, with relatively modest incomes, to enter their retirement absolutely debt free. In the interim they paid off a house, gave their only child an education, and traveled a good portion of the world.

Michelle is clearly not the culprit. She, as I said, was a good money manager before we met. If anyone is a corrupter here, it is me.

How about some trauma of youth? Maybe I was teased for having shabby clothes and vowed never to be teased again.

Nope. No clothes-related bullying.

In fact, as a kid, I was pretty good with money. I remember buying my own set of hockey equipment (this might be a false memory, but I'm clinging to it like grim death). When I was twelve, my dad split the cost of a nearly dead pickup truck. It cost me $200, a princely sum for a twelve-year-old, but that $200 of savings represented a giant leap toward adulthood, a ritual passage epitomized by rust and a bad clutch (you simply don't get a premium vehicle for $400). By the way, I know that twelve sounds like an incredibly young age at which to be a vehicle owner. All I can say in explanation is that where I came from, having a pickup was a bit of a rite of passage, and my dad was the kind of guy who liked to include his son in things. When I was just a year older, I bought my mom a necklace and my dad a 35-millimeter camera for Christmas (all with my own savings). That camera lasted longer than my skill with money.

But, of course, I really do know the answer. I understand the root of my lack of monetary success. In fact, I can almost state the date, hour, and place of my economic demise. I was twenty-two years old. I had just graduated from college. I was planning a trip to Europe, and as part of my preparations, I had obtained my first credit card. Oh, woe is the day that demon plastic fouled my financial soul.

I can still picture the card. It was silver with red lettering. It was a bit of an epiphany that you could obtain credit without actually having a credit history (this was the late 1980s, just before the era of family pets getting unsolicited credit cards in the mail). I was tempted to go out and use it immediately, but instead I stored it safely in my wallet and went about my business. If only it had stayed that way.

One night, exhausted from long hours and little sleep, I ventured out for a beer or two with some coworkers. The beer tasted good, there were pretty girls around, and the band was passable. Two beers turned into six, and soon I noticed my cash getting dangerously low. Remembering my newly acquired credit card, I decided that another round was in order. I'd pay off the card in the morning.

By 1 a.m. I was Nelson Rockefeller (I would have been Paris Hilton, but she was only eight at the time and completely unknown to me—it was a simpler time). The drinks were flowing, and I was buying. It felt good to be rich. I was generous and munificent. Had you been with me that night, I would have happily bought you a drink. I bought one for everyone.

It was only in the harsh light of morning (and it was undoubtedly very harsh that morning) that I realized my folly. But it was too late, in more ways than one. I had been introduced to consumer debt, and like a subprime mortgage lender, I could not be swayed from my new lifestyle, even by the certainty of financial disaster.

I am not the worst culprit in North America (not by a long shot, given what has happened of late), but I have done my share to perpetuate our debt-driven economy.

All of this is simply a preface to my assertion that I knew Frugality would prove to be one of the most difficult aspects of Franklin's course of virtues for me. I had no doubt that my table of vices would be filled to overflowing by the end of the week. At the same time, it presented unique opportunities. Like Order, it presented a real visceral opportunity for improvement. Frugality speaks of the concrete. Spend less money—what could be simpler?

And there is more here than even Order offered. All of the virtues up to this point could be slanted in a manner that allowed for success no matter your (my) actual accomplishment. Frugality, on the other hand, at least if taken literally, is very specific. Did you make no expense other than that which would benefit you or others? Do the math. I have nowhere to go but up.

A Day of Tea Bags

On the night before Frugality began, as I was getting ready for work, I considered how I might put Frugality to work immediately.

Unfortunately, the best I could come up with was tea bags.

On most days, like millions of North Americans, I begin my workday with a cup of steaming coffee purchased at a price far greater than that paid to the producer and contained in a cup that is slowly killing our planet. But today, on the first day of Frugality, I would break the iron grip of java, strike a blow for Al Gore, and brew my own tea. A simple plastic baggy (must remember to reuse that—Al would be mad if I didn't) full of tea bags transported to my work would help avoid my inevitable purchase of a coffee at our local canteen. I loaded the bag the night before Day 1 and set it on the counter for the next morning.

Michelle, ever observant of my behavior, looked at the tea bags, then fixed me with one of those glares that said, "I know what you're doing. Watch yourself."

In the morning, as I gathered up my stash of tea, I mentioned that Frugality was the virtue of the week. Michelle pointed at me as if I had admitted my part in the Kennedy assassination and said, "Aha! I knew it." She shook her finger.

I am trying, I explained to her. I am being Frugal, I told her proudly, because Ben says that we should make no expense but that which will benefit ourselves or others. Michelle turned away, a slightly sad look on her face, and said, "So it takes some dead guy to tell you what I've been trying to tell you for fifteen years? That's a little hard on the ego."

As she walked away, I was reminded of a mantra taught to me by an old girlfriend. This might be a good time to say it. Ready? Here goes:

"Men are stupid!"

I knew my wife had been telling me for years to be more careful with money. How could I not know? She tells me nearly every day. So did I throw her a bone and give her credit for my attempted change? Nooooo. I gave all the glory to a guy two hundred years past caring.

"Men are stupid!"

If you forget this little ditty, just ask the nearest woman. Many know it by heart.

Notwithstanding my wife's slight bitterness at Ben's influence on my life, I trundled off to work secure in the knowledge that I had at least taken a first step in being more frugal. It took some will-power, upon arriving at my office, not to make my usual trip to the cafeteria to buy a coffee and muffin. But I was able to refrain, saving $1.87 and enough fat content to add an extra hour to my life.

As I contemplated my newfound, if modest, Frugality, I filled the electric kettle Michelle had long ago purchased and plugged it in to await the first concrete benefit of Ben's fifth virtue. And then I learned my second lesson for the day: Kettles don't always work. The concrete, tangible benefit of this virtue, within my grasp only moments before, had been dashed by some quirk of electronics. As I stared stupidly at my now useless kettle, one of my colleagues happened by and asked helpfully, "Doesn't work?" I resisted the urge to breach the virtue of Tranquillity.

My tea kettle malfunction was clearly a product of bad karma.

Shortly before my problems with the kettle, I had been faced with an ethical dilemma and perhaps made the wrong choice. There is a young woman I see on the bus almost every morning. I take note of her because almost every morning when she steps on the bus, she announces to the bus driver that she has forgotten her student ID (on my local transit system, high school students ride free). I had noticed, of late, that a number of the bus drivers had dressed her down and told her, as they let her on board, that this was the last time. None, in the end, follow through on the threat. I've begun to wonder if she is, in fact, a student. I have waited, I must admit with shame, with some anticipation for one of the bus drivers to finally follow through on his threat not to grant her passage. On this, the first morning of my Frugality challenge, I was rewarded.

The bus driver in question, the gruffest of his number, refused to let her on the bus.

As I looked at the young woman, standing at the door of the bus, my inner Franklin raged in battle. On one hand, my curmudgeonly side enjoyed watching this young woman finally receive her comeuppance. Either her fraudulent bus riding had been discovered, or her poor morning preparations had been her undoing. "Serves ya right," my judgmental inner voice screamed out. On the other hand, I saw that her face was red from the cold, and my better angels, those I hoped I was freeing with this course of virtue, said, "Go buy her a ride with your bus pass." Before the clear winner could be found in my inner struggle, the man behind her, a frequent bus companion of mine, pulled out his pass and announced that he would pay for her ride.

It was then, I think, that Ben decided to punish me with the kettle.

I'd like to say that my inner struggle arose from a genuine uncertainly about what the right thing to do had been. But even if there was some legitimate dichotomy of opinion on the right choice generally, I knew what the right choice was for me. A smug, condemnatory righteousness should never win out (at least in my mind) over a generous heart. That it did, even if only through hesitation, meant that I had a long way to go.

Here's the bigger problem. In this week of Frugality, I realized I had missed some of the point. Ben's Frugality is not entirely about spending less money. I should have known this. Chris told me that Franklin was seeking more Samaritan (the good kind) than Scrooge. He wanted, through Frugality, to give benefit to others. Some commentators on Franklin's course have noted the absence of any virtue like Charity. In doing so they had missed the point of Frugality, just as I had. This Frugality is all about Charity.

I would like to say that I wanted the errant bus user to be taught a lesson, and I suppose that was true, yet "Scrooge" would have been the best word to describe my attitude on the bus. Ebenezer is me. One punch on a rider card and I would have benefited others with my spending, done what Franklin called a *good* for the day, and demonstrated a deeper understanding of Ben's path to righteousness.

{ Beware of little expenses. A small leak will sink a great ship. }

Ah, well. No sense in peaking too early.

If Tea Bags Don't Work, Try Eggs

I am the king of the eleven-minute omelet. I'm not sure what the previous world record for the preparation, cooking, and consumption of the three-cheese omelet was, but surely I have beaten the record. In my quest to be frugal, I decided that I would replace my usual, aforementioned, and much-loved morning coffee and muffin with an omelet before I left for work. Healthier, wealthier, and wiser. It was positively Franklinian.

The problem was that I made this decision immediately after putting my two youngest children on a school bus and exactly eleven minutes before my city bus was to arrive at my nearby bus stop. Undeterred by Michelle's expressions of doubt, I busily cracked, beat, and chopped my way to a hearty and frugal breakfast. With one eye on the clock, I managed to slide the omelet from the frying pan a full two minutes before I had to run to catch my bus. Unfortunately, I noticed as I slid the omelet from pan to plate that I had slightly undercooked my breakfast. No problem—another thirty seconds in the microwave not only solved the cooking problem but also fluffed the omelet somewhat—perhaps I had inadvertently arrived at a new omelet cooking method. There was no end to the benefits of Ben's course of virtues.

As I pulled my creation from the microwave with still over a minute to go before I had to catch the bus, I encountered yet another problem: The omelet was now too hot to eat. Panic rising in my throat, I eyed the clock and then the omelet and then the clock again. Finally, I stuffed the steaming omelet into my mouth and discovered why one should not cook an omelet in the microwave. It was the approximate temperature of the surface of the sun.

Despite the heat and the pain, I shoveled the last of the omelet down my scorched throat and noticed that it was now two minutes past the time that I normally left for my bus. I raced down the stairs, jumped into my shoes, pulled on my overcoat, grabbed my gym bag and briefcase, and rushed to the bus stop. As I turned the corner, I caught a glimpse of the back end of my bus pulling away down the street.

So there I stood with a burnt tongue, untied shoes, and a depressing certainty that I had missed my bus. So far I had been defeated in Frugality by tea bags and eggs. If I was not being frugal, I was at least exploring the basic food groups.

It struck me, as my tongue throbbed with pain, that I was enjoying Franklin's course (notwithstanding the physical injuries). It was fun and amusing to pay so much attention to my own behavior, even when the behavior was not virtuous. Perhaps I was enjoying it too much. Just as I had let myself drift off into folly, I was reminded that Ben's virtues, on occasion, carry a more serious tone. The death, in custody, of one of the defendants I most commonly encountered as a prosecutor forced me to consider my own feelings about his passing.

This was a man with whom I had been dealing since before my

days as a prosecutor, stretching well back into my time as a barroom bouncer. He was to me, in many ways, the enemy. A career criminal, his downward spiral of drug use, violence, and illicit conduct could have led him to no end but that which he met. He was nonetheless a human being. He left, to my knowledge, a mother and a son, and surely others to mourn his passing. He was to them, I'm sure, more than the continual menace that he was to the rest of society. If I was truly following Ben's course of virtues and adhering in the best way to his precepts, I would at the very least not take pleasure in this man's death. Surrounded by the black humor that is so prevalent in the criminal justice world, it was difficult not to succumb to the notion that the world was a better place without this man. But I tried. I attempted to think of him as more than an inevitable statistic. Small comfort, no doubt, to his grieving mother. I resolved to remember to not always be so flippant.

On a happier note, one of my colleagues celebrated a milestone birthday. She had made it clear to me and others in the office that she wanted no recognition of this birthday. We promptly ignored that request, and our support staff prepared a cake to mark the occasion. The problem was that this coworker would have, if she had known about the existence of the cake, run screaming in the other direction.

It fell to me to deceive her into coming into my office. I found it interesting to discover how easy it was for me to fall into a pattern of deception. I *{ Creditors have better memories than debtors.}* simply picked up the phone, called her office, and said, "I've got gossip; you need to come here." Even more interesting was my colleague's reaction. I almost did not have enough time to hang up the phone before she appeared in my doorway, checked in midstride by the birthday cake with cream cheese frosting on my desk and the entire staff assembled. I remarked that she was incredibly quick when she thought I had some gossip for her. She answered with a one-fingered thank-you.

Deception, sarcasm, digital profanity. Franklin's virtues abounded.

Frugality Versus Loyalty

Despite coming to the conclusion that this virtue had more to do with the commonwealth than my personal wealth, I decided that my wife's esteem of me might be served by concentrating on our own Frugality. This would need some focus on expenses larger than tea bags.

If I was going to be frugal, I decided I needed to take things proactively. Saving a dollar here or a dollar there might add up over time, but it was clear to me that if I really wanted to save money, I needed to attack our big expenses. My biggest expense every month is, of course, the mortgage. I say "of course" because it seems Everest-like even to consider being mortgage free, and the thought of those who have scaled this particular summit fill me with wonder and, sadly, envy.

Though the value of my house increases almost weekly in the mini–housing boom we are experiencing in my subdivision, I see no immediate benefit from it. Instead, I watch as a sizable portion of every one of my paychecks slides effortlessly through my hands and right into the greedy paws of the banking industry. So, considering how many coffee and muffin purchases I devote to my housing costs, it strikes me that any effort to minimize these payments is a blow well struck for Frugality.

Of course, if life were that easy, we wouldn't need bank bailouts. Problem No. 1 was that my mortgage was only at midlife. I was two and a half years into the five-year term, and I knew that any effort to change my mortgage would result in a significant penalty. I know this because I've tried it before (which might provide further insight on the whole me versus Frugality struggle).

Problem No. 2 was that I feel immensely uncomfortable any-time I even consider haggling over money. I know people for whom the chance to banter and bargain is akin to sex. I, on the other hand, break out in hives at the thought of financial negotiations. I'd rather give something away than sell it, and if I had to bargain for my salary, I'd be working for free.

This, however, was a week of improvement. This was a week to set aside fear and embrace Frugality. This was a week when I could blame things on Ben. I made an initial call to my bank.

Problem No. 3 turned out to be talking to a real human. Actu-ally, as I listened to the menu of voice mail options, it occurred to me that this might be the one time when I didn't mind the imper-sonal touch. Sadly, it's much easier for me to talk to an unresponsive machine when discussing finances. With some trepidation, I left a message indicating that I was concerned with the rate of interest I was paying, and asked for a payout on my mortgage including any penalty.

There—at least I had made a call. That would be enough to say that I had made an attempt, and now I could crawl back under my financial rock and pretend that I had been virtuous. Apparently, however, my phone message set off minor tremors in the financial industry.

A representative from the bank returned my call, sounding somewhat desperate. An appointment was immediately set up, in-troductions were made to a new financial adviser, and a closed-door meeting led to a number of proposed next steps. It was an interesting and instructive look into, at the very least, my bank and perhaps the financial services industry as a whole.

I can't imagine that losing my minuscule business would have caused my massive bank's stock value to take an immediate tumble. Notwithstanding this, as a result of just one simple inquiry, I was being fawned over. As we bantered back and forth over what was best for my financial health, one of the advisers said, "Don't worry, whatever happens, we're going to give you a lower rate and save you money." I felt like Donald Trump—with better hair and no reality show (okay, maybe not better hair).

This, I must say, was a bit of a revelation to me. For the first time in any of my dealings with a banking institution, it actually seemed like I had some leverage. Maybe I just caught them on a bad day. Perhaps I simply found two banking officials sincerely interested in my financial well-being. Or just as likely, the bank was beginning to feel the pinch of the competition in the financial services industry across the continent. Whatever the reason, the dictate to be frugal was paying off.

I had been so successful at the bank, I decided that other fixed expenses merited some attention. Insurance, lawn care, long-distance plans—they were all subject to my newfound consumer empowerment.

And then came the guilt.

The problem with this new feeling of financial empowerment was that it was butting up against one of the virtues that Franklin never mentions, a virtue that my parents attempted to instill by example. I was taught to be loyal. Loyalty to family, loyalty to community, loyalty to country. Less logically, I was also taught to be loyal to the places where, and the people with whom, I conduct business. People of my parents' generation drove the same brand of car throughout their life, they shopped at the same stores, and they banked at the same bank. As I sat down with two banking officials, relatively unknown to me, in an institution to whom I am just a number, and discussed how we could find a middle ground that allowed me to keep more of my money and them to keep any of it, it occurred to me that I was being disloyal.

I was like some star athlete in the midst of a good season seeking a new contract. I was trying to renegotiate.

Worse, I wasn't even a star. In the financial world, I was a career minor leaguer. I had never said that I would take my business elsewhere, I was unfailingly polite, and I truly appreciated the efforts that the banking officials were making for me . . . and yet . . . I was still looking for cash. I hadn't even had a good season.

What would Ben say? Could Ben have even contemplated the nature of our modern economy? He was, of course, a very successful businessman and was shrewd in his enterprises to the extent that he effectively "retired" young, freeing his time and talents for science, politics, and eventually nation building. Perhaps he would say, to my early mortgage renegotiation, "It's about time." Or perhaps he would shake his head in disapproval. This, fortunately, was one instance in those thirteen weeks that it mattered not one iota what Ben would or would not have wanted. Michelle was happy, and Michelle trumps Ben. She is alive and much better looking.

Be Wary of Franklin Followers Bearing Gifts

As my encounter with Frugality drew to a close, I was mindful of two things: (1) I probably spent no less money than I have in any other week; and (2) I did little good for others with whatever Frugality I practiced. Of the first I was not much concerned. While I may have spent no less, I probably spent no more. In an age of consumerism and materialism, simply stemming the tide of purchases may, in fact, be a small victory.

At least not until Problem No. 2 arises.

Franklin was subtler than I had first imagined. Let me explain with a little criticism of the great man, not from me but from those who know him best.

Franklin, notwithstanding the great affection Americans feel for him, is not without his detractors, and his virtue course has come under considerable scrutiny. Maybe that's what happens when you dare to suggest you tried to be "morally perfect." The critics have questioned the rationale for the virtues, the particular virtues selected, and his success in achieving his goal. And the critics are not Ben haters—at least not all of them. Most are fans, men and women who have devoted a good portion of their own lives to a study of our hero.

Take Edmund Morgan. Mr. Morgan is, according to the author bio on his book *Benjamin Franklin*, Sterling Professor of History Emeritus at Yale University and is cited as "one of America's most distinguished historians." The Yale History Faculty's website quotes a student as saying: "Morgan doesn't teach history, he narrates it. Listening to his lectures is like listening to a story." Even the picture of Morgan on the dust jacket of his book reveals a man whom no one could find disagreeable. And he clearly loves Ben Franklin. His affection for his subject pours out in the first words of his book. So here we have a gifted writer, scholar, and teacher who has a genuine affection for Franklin, and he is a likable guy in his own right. What does he think of Franklin's course of virtues?

Morgan describes Franklin's choice of virtues as a "puzzle," and he says that it is "as interesting for what it leaves out as for what it includes."[1] While conceding that the virtues pass the test of "usefulness," Morgan contends that their usefulness has a character of self-centeredness, in contrast to Franklin's own character as well as his other writings and actions. He regards the bulk of the virtues as aimed at personal happiness and the remainder as morally ambiguous.

Other observers have called the project "odd,"[2] "not to the modern taste,"[3] and "not heroic."[4]

Not heroic? Self-centeredness? That's harsh.

And more than harsh, the critics may just be plain wrong. While Frugality might smack of self-centeredness, it might just as well be grounded in Charity, as I suggested above. Is giving money away not an expense that benefits others? Are Charity and Frugality not inextricably linked? I think Franklin's critics sell him short.

If they criticized me, on the other hand, they'd be right on the money (so to speak). Even though I recognized the altruistic aspects of the virtue, I failed to practice them, at least not in any extravagant way.

I was mindful, however, that even small acts of generosity can be meaningful. I gave money to a panhandler specifically because it was the week of Frugality. Hardly Mother Teresa–like, I admit, but it felt good. Even in such minor acts of generosity, however, one must exercise some caution.

Chris had suggested that as part of Frugality I practice "random acts of generosity." As an example, he proposed that at some point I buy a coffee for the next person in line at a coffee shop. Flush with the Franklinian notion of Frugality, I decided to give it a try. One morning as I stood paying for my morning coffee and muffin (yes, I was back to the coffee and muffin—let's just say I'm omelet shy), I handed the cashier double the price.

Signaling to the person behind me, I said, "Let me buy that next person's breakfast." The cashier shrugged and moved on to serve my beneficiary. For a moment, I felt good.

My self-satisfaction at this tiny act of generosity quickly disappeared, however, when I noticed that the customer behind me seemed to have taken my gesture the wrong way. I'm a long way from the days of flirting, but there was little to mistake in her slightly downcast eyes, the fluttering of her lashes, the coy smile, and her tiny wave.

As I caught myself in the midst of waving back, I realized, in horror, that she had taken my Franklinian gesture of Frugality/ Charity as a come-on. Like a puppy caught stealing food from the cupboard, I looked left and right for the nearest exit and scurried off in fear.

So, the lesson here is that if you are going to be spontaneously charitable, ensure that you are not suspected of ulterior motives. On the upside, if you are in the dating market, it seems a coffee and a muffin are good icebreakers.

FRUGALITY

MAKE NO EXPENSE BUT TO DO GOOD TO OTHERS OR YOURSELF, I.E., WASTE NOTHING.							
	S	M	T	W	Th	F	Sat
Temperance	★★★		★	★★		★	★
Silence		★			★	★	
Order	★	★				★	
Resolution	★		★				★
Frugality		★	★		★	★	
Industry	★★	★					★
Sincerity		★				★	
Justice		★		★			
Moderation							★
Cleanliness	★	★		★			
Tranquillity		★				★	★
Chastity							
Humility	★	★★	★	★	★	★	★

{CHAPTER 6}

Industry

Lose no time; be always employed in something useful; cut off all unnecessary actions

HERE IS ONE OF MY FAVORITE STORIES OF BEN FRANKLIN. FOR MORE than a decade leading up to the American Revolution, Franklin had been America's point guy in the mother country. He was the representative for several of the colonial assemblies, he had made the case for a peaceful reconciliation between England and her colonies, and he had raised the world's consciousness about the not-yet-born country. More than anything, Franklin wanted America (or what would become America) to remain part of the British Empire, but not at any cost. Eventually, it became apparent to Franklin that matters had come to a head, and in March 1775 he finally saw the end of any hope and left for home. It must have been a desperate trip. He

{ *A life of leisure and a life of laziness are two things. There will be sleeping enough in the grave.* }

was going back to an uncertain future, he had failed in his role in England, and his wife had died the year before in his absence. So what did Franklin do on the journey home?

He discovered the Gulf Stream (well, sort of).

Instead of moping or pouting or despairing, Franklin took the temperature of the water as he crossed the Atlantic. He had already developed a chart of the Gulf Stream in 1769 with his cousin Timothy Folger, but he used this most depressing of trips to confirm and explain his earlier work. In a word, he was industrious.

Were that I was so.

When I think of Industry, I remember the day we got cable television.

Like Gabriel announcing the Virgin birth, it was a revelation. There may even have been an angelic hallelujah chorus (at least in my mind).

The details are burned into my memory. A small box was installed atop our bulky television, its digital readout like something from the space program. I can see my father fiddling with the remote control searching for the right channel (this was predictive—he's been playing with television remotes constantly since that moment). And then there it was: my first cable television program. Feel the heart thumping faster, cue the chorus, rise and join in the call. Hallelujah!

It was *The Jetsons*.

Up to that point *The Jetsons* was like kissing a girl: something I had heard about at school but never experienced. Yet with the twist of a coaxial wire and the click of a remote, my universe went from two fuzzy, rabbit-ear-captured stations to a multichannel bonanza (well, I think we were hauling in a maximum of ten, maybe twelve, signals with out first cable feed, but that seemed like a viewing

smorgasbord at the time). And unlike perhaps any media intervention before or since, my introduction to the joys of cable television
changed my world.

Before cable I was a rugged, self-entertaining, athletic child (at
least that's my memory). After a cable signal broadcast from WLBZ
Channel 2 in Bangor, Maine, however, I was lost in the exotic world
of afternoon soap operas, television sitcoms, and Eddie Driscoll and
The Great Money Movie. From the moment I came home from
school until supper, my world was consumed by television.

I even became a momentary star myself as an audience member
on a show called *Dick Stacey's Country Jamboree*, a gloriously bad
musical variety show filmed in the basement of Dick's motel. Anyone
could get up, without audition, and have a go. Viewers all over New
England and Eastern Canada were entranced (or aghast) as an eclec-
tic group of performers took the stage. Dick sponsored the show as
an advertisement for his gas stations. His famous tag line from the
commercials interspersed throughout the show was: "See these hands?
These hands pump gas and they stink." This was quality fare.

Somehow, during the run of Dick's musical showcase, my parents and I found ourselves as both visitors to Bangor and guests at
Dick's motel. After supper that night, Mom and Dad decided that
we'd take in a live performance of the *Country Jamboree*. Things
progressed as one might expect until, to my thirteen-year-old
amazement and horror, the host stopped beside me during his me-
anderings. I'm not sure what he asked me—probably where I was
from—nor am I sure how I replied. All I knew, and I was keenly
aware of it even as I was being interviewed, was that I had officially
been on television. Cable television. Cable television that was seen
in my hometown. The only long-term effect is a mild phobia about
being interviewed on camera (which has lasted to this day).

Television has played a significantly diminished role in my life as I've aged, both by choice and as a result of increasing demands on my time. There is no more Eddie Driscoll; he passed on after a battle with Alzheimer's not long ago. The *Jamboree* has long since been retired, and you can't even get the Bangor channels where I live. But television is still the siren that calls me onto the rocks of lethargy and slothfulness.

I am not alone. According to the American Academy of Pediatrics, American children watch an average of three to fours hours of television daily, and by the time they reach seventy, they will have watched seven to ten years of television.[1]

As a parent, it is frightening to see how thoroughly television has invaded our lives. It is the background noise of existence. If our forefathers lived to the murmur of the forests or the drone of industry, our ambient noise is cable news, a laugh track, and an endless stream of ShamWow commercials.

Most modern criticism of television has focused on the effect that it has on younger viewers. Anyone who has seen a six-year-old stare, slack-jawed and droopy-eyed, at the screen for more than five minutes understands this concern. But how much time is lost by *adults* with that same glazed-over stare?

I am not, of course, advocating a ban on television. But somewhere between *Dick Stacey's Country Jamboree* and *American Idol*, it occurred to me that at the very least I should feel guilty about my viewing habits. Other than a few memories of the famous people of Maine, what have I gained from watching TV? Certainly no one, Benjamin Franklin in particular, would call my TV viewing hours "industrious."

And so, as part of my week of Industry, I decided to change my viewing habits. I thought that I might convince my family to join me, but coming so close on the heels of Frugality, I decided to avoid a family coup d'état and restrict this virtue to myself.

I also chose not to impose a complete prohibition. Mindful of one of the upcoming virtues, I decided to do this in Moderation. I resolved to limit my TV viewing to no more than one hour per day. I would use my time that had in the past been devoted to an absence of Industry to surround myself in a blanket of Franklin's middle virtues. I would become industrious.

See these hands? These hands write books.

One Is the Loneliest Number

By the end of Day 1, I felt like I had the DTs.

Like many assessments of my capabilities, I badly overestimated my ability to withstand the lure of television. I assumed, given that I don't watch that much television, that I would saunter through the day almost oblivious to my own commitment.

Oh, did I say I'd watch only an hour a day? I'd forgotten. Nothing to me really.

Ha! Never was an hour more thought about, never was unfettered access to a television more coveted. I was like an inmate waiting for telephone access. Every few seconds I reached for the remote, stopping only when I remembered that it was verboten. I was fidgety and anxious. Worse than that, rather than being a wedge in the door of Industry as I had hoped, my program of television abstinence was becoming a hindrance to any productivity. I thought that when not watching TV, I would be doing something useful. Instead, all my intellectual energy was being expended on trying not to think about the fact that I was not to be watching television. I felt like a crack addict in a convent.

Why was I having such difficulty? The answer was no real mystery. First, though I hadn't opted for total abstinence, I had treated this too much like TV detox. Ben Franklin clearly knew the dangers of complete denial—as I thought I had when I planned for an hour of television a night. Notwithstanding that, I was acting as if even a momentary glance at the remote would turn me into stone. The self-denial made me covetous.

My second problem was a familiar   {*Industry need not wish.*} one. Lack of preparation. I relied, to my detriment, on whatever had gotten me through the rest of my life—brains, chutzpah, cheese and crackers—to get me through my first day of self-imposed television restrictions. Bad idea.

Finally, I should have tried, even at the risk of serious injury, to involve my family in this adventure. Misery is often borne easier if shared. As it was, I was actively rebuffed in my efforts.

At some point during the evening, Michelle came into the living room, sat in her favorite chair, and noticed that I was sitting in silence, looking as if I were waiting for the dentist.

"What are you doing?" she asked.

"Not watching television. I've decided to be more industrious, and watching TV isn't useful."

She looked at me with the sort of weary expression only a spouse can display and sighed. "I thought we weren't supposed to be part of this. If you don't want to watch TV, go do it downstairs."

On Day 1, I could add *Banishment* to my list of accomplishments.

A Bad Week for Industry

Being a prosecutor in a small town is like being an emergency room physician. You need to have a firm grasp on almost every different type of situation that might present itself, be flexible in your thought processes, get used to the sight of a little blood, and be prepared for some dry spells. My community is very safe. However, there are still enough impaired drivers, wife beaters, shoplifters, convenience store burglars, and occasional murderers to keep all of the local prosecutors in court almost every day during the week. Each day presents a new challenge. My day runs from the tragic to the ridiculous, from the peculiar to the perverse. It is, however, as I said, very rarely boring.

One minute your victim is demanding the accused's blood, the next they are kissing in the hallway and pronouncing their undying love for each other. A witness one day is an accused the next, and there never seems to be a shortage of things that can go wrong immediately before a trial begins.

In short, those of us in the criminal justice system tend to be seat-of-the-pants types. We thrive on in-the-moment pressure and are not necessarily what you would call self-starters.

As bad luck would have it, my week of Industry coincided with a very slow week for the court system—the midwinter break. Thus, few trials, hearings, or other court activity. How could I be industrious, how could I follow Franklin's dictate to "Lose no time; be always employed in something useful; cut off all unnecessary actions" when the fates had taken away the very thing that drives my productivity in the first place?

My wise friend Chris had warned me, in our discussions on Industry, not to lose important achievements by being "too busy." His was an admonition not to lose the moments in the drive.

Maybe I am just too thick to understand. Or perhaps I am too simple to view the admonition to be industrious as anything but a call to work. Whatever the reason, I decided that I would take Franklin's words literally. I would ensure that I was always employed in something useful.

When I had finished my preparations for the next day's cases, I knew I needed to remain engaged. I needed to do something that would benefit myself and others. I looked around, drumming my fingers on my desk (at least metaphorically), and wondered exactly *what* would be a benefit.

I could prepare for future cases, but that seemed too pedestrian. I might work on my book, but given that I was contemplating Industry during work hours—on the taxpayer's nickel, so to speak— whatever I did should at least be a benefit to said taxpayers. I was at a loss.

You might think, given that the week was to be devoted to Industry and Order and Resolution had already passed, that I might be better prepared. All I can say to such naiveté is that you haven't been paying attention.

Finally, unsure of how else to be industrious, I decided to create a practice manual for prosecutors doing criminal appeals. In the end it was more assembling than creating. When I prepare for appeals, I create checklists for procedures—annotated Rules of Court—and anticipate potential judicial questions. In my efforts to "be always employed in something useful," I compiled these materials, did some editing, and developed a guide for my fellow prosecutors. While I didn't complete it in one day, I was off to a reasonable start.

Had I been industrious? Well, I'm sure the manual will prove useful, but I have a sense that Franklin was hoping for something grander. After all, he was an inventor, a creator. He didn't simply assemble the Franklin stove—he gave it life. His bifocals were not some lame conglomeration of earlier pairs of glasses. Franklin's Industry was purposeful and directed and inventive.

Industry in the Franklinian sense has, I think, less to do with simply being busy and more to do with getting busy. As Chris said to me in his lead-up to the week, "It is not in the nose-to-thegrindstone busy-ness that we find truth. It is in the small gestures of understanding and compassion, the little distractions, that we shine."

I think Franklin's notion of being busy was tied up in his desire to do good works, to be a benefit to others. My little appeal manual might have been a start, but I could do better.

Of all the virtues, this is the one (so far) for which I have the most affinity. Indeed, Industry was what I was hoping for when I started this project. Or, more precisely, it was the absence of this from my life that drove me on. Guilt is a great motivator.

We've lost perspective. We, in the West, are simply so privileged that we no longer have a true sense of sacrifice and hardship. Now before some guy who lost his job at an assembly plant and had his home taken from him loads up his shotgun and tries to find my house on Google Maps, hear me out. Even in our most desperate times, a nostalgic look back at the good old days is fiction. Life might have been simpler before, but it was also exponentially more difficult. Beyond those in abject poverty, even the poor in modern North America have luxuries and conveniences of which our ancestors could not have dreamt.

What we have lost with this relative affluence is a sense of self-sufficiency. That is one of the motivations behind Benjamin Franklin's admonition to be industrious—a drive to be self-reliant. The other is something Franklin displayed in abundance: selflessness. It is the paucity of these in my own life and the abundance of these in Franklin's that make this the most personally appealing of the virtues. When I think of Industry, beyond my earlier reference to television, I think of my grandfather.

So, for the rest of this week, I decided this would be the week of . . .

Big Haze

My mother's father, Hazen Wood Dickson (or Big Haze, as we call him at the annual golf tournament named in his honor), was not a man of means. Indeed, I would say for a good portion of his life he was poor. He always worked and worked hard, but he never earned much money. Despite this, he raised a happy and close-knit family and left a considerable legacy. He was also the most self-reliant man I have ever known. In fact, though he holds no patents, and no royalty checks from licensing schemes pad the coffers of his estate, he was much like Franklin: an inventor.

Tread on the concrete walkway from his driveway to his house and you'd never be encumbered by snow or ice. He created a self-cleaning walkway using steam generated from a woodstove. His pantry was accessible by a trapdoor that was raised or lowered by an electronic pulley system, which might not have been revolutionary, or an invention at all, but was very impressive to a ten-year-old boy. My grandmother told me he invented the world's first self-loading pulpwood truck and that he would have been rich if he had thought to find a partner with business acumen. He had a backyard filled with ancient single-stroke engines and portable sawmills run by steam motors, and I never saw him turn to a mechanic, plumber, carpenter, or handyman for assistance. It was others who turned to him.

For me there was a little bit of Franklin in my grandfather, particularly his Industry. He was always busy, never idle, and he did it for the love of doing it, and perhaps to make the world a little better. There are lessons there for me. That is why I decided that the week of Industry should be Big Haze week: a week of invention.

For a time I considered actually trying to invent something. I've always been fascinated by the notion of creating something new. Fascination, however, does not equal creation. The truth is that I am simply not my grandfather or Benjamin Franklin. If I was going to be original, I would need to look a little closer to home. The appeal manual was in the right ballpark but not quite, well, inventive enough. I needed something new, original, beneficial, and industrious. I needed to do something no one else had done.

One of the most time-consuming jobs for police and prosecutors is obtaining a search warrant. It is, of course, essential, both in a practical sense and constitutionally. No one, certain exceptions aside, should have his or her privacy invaded unless a judge agrees beforehand. The process is, however, laborious and frustrating. First, we expect police officers to draft documents that will stand up to judicial scrutiny despite the fact that they generally have little, if any, legal training. Second, we expect them to draft the documents requesting a warrant in the dynamic environment of a criminal investigation. Prosecutors help, but the real burden falls on the police. This was the perfect opportunity for an "invention." This, I reasoned, was more like Ben (and Big Haze): industrious.

I started planning a database for the preparation of warrants. It would automate the type of advice that I offer to police on a daily basis and help replicate the tombstone data that must be repeated in the affidavits used in warrant applications. I had visions of keystroke-saving measures, data replication, alerts when deadlines neared. It would be glorious. It would be inventive. It would be industrious.

It would be . . . a long process.

I quickly realized that I was not going to finish this project in a day, or a week, or a month. I contacted some friends in the IT field, and we came up with some relatively unsophisticated templates, which made it clear that this was a project that would require a long-term commitment. At this point, my desire to be industrious ran headlong into my terribly short attention span. If Industry takes more than twenty minutes, I am in trouble; twenty minutes is my "sit still" limit. I once heard someone suggest that conversations have a twenty-minute life span. That is, every conversation has a lull or pause or dead spot approximately every twenty minutes. It seems also to apply to my working life. Absent some external restriction, I have to rise and take a short walk every twenty minutes.

On another day, that might have been the end of my warrant preparation database. I might have chucked the whole idea and gone back to my slothful ways. But this week I was in the hands of Benjamin Franklin. This week I was dedicated to Industry. So despite my recognition of my twenty-minute attention span, I resolved that I would remain industrious. I resolved that every time I felt like getting up at the twenty-minute mark, I would remind myself that Ben insists we be always employed in something useful—not always *except for twenty-minute stretch breaks*. I knew I would not finish the warrant preparation software before the end of the week, but I also knew that I would not give up.

I think Ben was actually having some effect on me. By the end of the workweek, Ben's virtue of Industry seemed to have helped. I had found that I was indeed more industrious that week. I had completed my appeal manual, made substantial inroads on my warrant database, finalized arrangements for a golf trip, and furthered my plans for the pro bono charity.

{ *It is the working man who is the happy man. It is the idle man who is the miserable man.* }

Okay, so I hadn't invented an odometer, mapped the Gulf Stream, or created the armonica (all things, you might have guessed, done or invented by Ben Franklin . . . and yes, again, there is no *h* . . . I don't think Franklin had anything to do with the harmonica). I had, however, been doing useful things in the small sense. Baby steps, I told myself, baby steps.

The Industry of Rest

If television is the enemy of virtue, it has two allies that are almost as effective at killing Franklin's notion of Industry.

The first is simply the nature of the modern family. As with every generation before us, today's parents strive to give their kids every opportunity they had growing up. The difference now is that my generation, having grown up in the 1970s and '80s, had a whole lot of opportunities. So when we want to give our children a better life, we've got some work to do.

Thus, the Industry of the modern family: the dance classes, piano lessons, and swim classes, soccer, basketball, and hockey. There are art classes and play dates. How about a foreign language? I think the BlackBerry was invented just so parents could keep up with their children's schedules.

One can debate the relative merits of this hyperbusy lifestyle, but what is certain is that it does not engender Industry from the parents. Who has time to invent a self-contained stove when soccer practice is over only ten minutes before swimming lessons? The only things that get created in that environment are fatigue, strife, and burnout. That, surely, is not Ben Franklin's idea of Industry.

The other creativity killer these days is the Internet. It is like a superhero gone bad—it was created for good, but it has turned to the forces of evil. Maybe that's an exaggeration, but I find the online world so compelling—so much information, so little time—that I have a hard time resisting its call. As captain of the good ship Industry, its siren call lures me onto the rocks of wasted time.

In any case, despite the challenges arrayed against me, the week of Industry was perhaps my most successful. I need not rehash my achievements, but it was the virtue to which I committed the most time and effort, and the reward was that the success is transferrable to the other virtues.

As a reward, instead of trying to cram more activities into our already busy family schedule, I did the most useful, industrious, and beneficial thing I had done all week: I relaxed with my family. We played games (I'm learning that even a seven-year-old can beat me at chess), read books, and went for walks. This was time well spent, not wasted. I'm sure Mr. Franklin would have approved.

About the TV thing. Like the junkie I had clearly become, the first few days were the hardest. The craving was almost physical; I was jonesing. By the end of the week, however, I was out of the woods. I didn't reach absently for the remote, the sound of the TV in the next room didn't cause Pavlovian salivation and a sudden craving for carbohydrates, and I didn't find myself wondering about what was on the History Channel at any given moment. I'm not claiming that I was on the wagon completely, but I didn't miss it— not much. Besides, I had committed to this television avoidance for only a week. The next week was Sincerity. During the week of Sincerity, I could admit that I liked a little useless, mind-numbing pastime. During the week of Sincerity, I could get back to the History Channel.

I just wouldn't watch as much. I was too busy trying to figure out how to beat a seven-year-old at chess.

INDUSTRY

LOSE NO TIME; BE ALWAYS EMPLOYED IN SOMETHING USEFUL; CUT OFF ALL UNNECESSARY ACTIONS.							
	S	M	T	W	Th	F	Sat
Temperance		★		★	★★		★
Silence	★			★	★		★
Order	★	★			★		
Resolution				★			
Frugality	★	★	★			★	★
Industry		★			★	★	
Sincerity				★			
Justice					★	★	
Moderation				★			★
Cleanliness	★	★		★		★	★
Tranquillity		★	★		★		★
Chastity							
Humility	★	★★	★	★★	★	★	

{CHAPTER 7}

Sincerity

*Use no hurtful deceit; think innocently and justly,
and if you speak, speak accordingly*

AT LONG LAST! I WAS ON MY OWN TURF. I KNEW THE SEAMS IN THE
floor, the bounce of the rim, the cast of the lights. I was no longer
playing in front of a hostile crowd. After a long road trip through the
minefield of Franklinian virtues, I finally had home field advantage.

The next three virtues had a recognizable, comfy blanket quality
for me. Sincerity, Justice, and Moderation. Finally, words that didn't
seem like they were written in some
long dead language. Temperance I can't
do, but I was all over Sincerity.

{ *Half a truth is often a
great lie.* }

What is that old saying? Pride goeth before the fall.

Honesty is one of the qualities that I most admire in myself and
others. In a world where lies and deception are part of some morally
ambiguous game plan for success, I treasure the truth. And it is not
even pure lies that fire my boiler. My ire is reserved for half-truths
and "plausible deniability." I cringe when I see people, the powerful

and the pathetic alike, twist information to create something that is not an outright lie but at least a distorted version of reality. This spin-doctored, language-massaged messaging is a symptom, in my crotchety view, of a denial of personal responsibility. Do you know how you spot a mistake in our modern world? Look for all the people trying to "distance" themselves from it.

I hope I have not set the bar too high here. I believe that I have developed a reputation, personally and professionally, as someone whose word can be trusted. I endeavor never to lie to my children, my spouse, my family, my friends, or even strangers . . . but . . . knowing that perfection, even in this limited virtue, is impossible, I acknowledge that I have transgressed this virtue on occasion. Some have been minor, some not so. Let me explain. (If you are under the age of twelve, read no further—there is information below that you do not want to know.)

ARE YOU STILL READING, TWELVE AND UNDERS? STOP, I IMPLORE YOU.

OKAY, ONLY ADULTS HERE? GOOD. NOW LISTEN CLOSELY, I HAVE A REV-elation of profound importance to our experiment.

There is no Santa Claus. There, I said it. But that's the most benign sort of deception.

On the more fundamental side of Sincerity, however, I have engaged in some significant acts of deception. For instance, for three months I did not tell my parents that I had been caught in a bar during a raid by liquor inspectors (you know the story from one of the earlier chapters . . . my parents had to wait longer for the truth). I was anxious to plead guilty, pay my fine, and pack this particular skeleton far back in my closet.

I know what you're thinking. A lie about Santa and underage drinking. That can't be the full extent of my deceptions. These really are the best lies I could recall. I really don't lie (okay, little white lies maybe, but we'll talk about that later). It's not that I am better or more moral than the average person. I am just really bad at lying.

Let me give you an example. I had to take transfer examinations to get admitted to the bar in my jurisdiction. The executive director of the law society left me and the two others taking the exam in a room with the tests and told us to leave them on the desk when we were finished. "You have three hours," he said as he left.

Well, I didn't finish in three hours. It took me a full half an hour extra, and by the time I laid my exam on the desk, I was breaking out in a cold sweat. No one would know how long it took me, I rationalized. It wasn't like I cheated, I told myself. By the time I reached my apartment, my conscience had taken hold of me, given me a good shake, and yelled, in its best conscience voice, "CONFESS!"

I called the law society. When I told the executive director what I had done, he laughed. "You think I care how long it took you?" he asked. "This isn't kindergarten. Don't worry about it."

But I had. I had worried about it. For the twenty minutes between my completion of the exam and my guilt-wracked telephone call, I had nearly had an aneurysm from worry. Lying is simply not for me. On the few occasions when I've managed to maintain a lie or deception for some period of time, the fates conspire against me. Remember how I was undone by a nasty little journalist sitting in the front row of the courtroom during my underage drinking story? That's what happens to me when I try to lie. It comes apart faster than a Sarah Palin interview on foreign policy.

So I am no saint, but I don't lie. My few feeble attempts at deception have led me to several core beliefs on Franklin's virtue of Sincerity. First, the truth is fundamental to the human community. Second, even truth is not an absolute. Third, no matter how hard you struggle against it, the truth will always come out. Fourth, don't trust small-town newspaper reporters (okay, that last one isn't very profound or perhaps even true, but I've held a two-decade-old grudge).

But here is a little more truth about truth.

We don't want it. And we don't engage in it. Not the bare, unmasked, whole truth. There is just no way we can handle it.

Can you imagine honest answers all the time? "How do I look in this dress?" *"It shows the fact that you've gained fifteen pounds in the last year."* "Do you think I'm losing my hair?" *"Losing? You hardly have any left to lose."*

I recently saw a reference to a study of forty thousand workers that found 93 percent of them admit to lying habitually and regularly in the workplace. Does it surprise you? How could it? We all lie (at least a little). The only thing the study shows is that 7 percent of the participants were lying.

SO WHY DO WE LIE? WE ARE SOCIALLY CONDITIONED TO LIE. WE reward and encourage deception. And maybe some of it isn't bad. Little white lies are what keep our relationships together, our workplaces tolerable, and our dinner parties interesting. Without them, people would be strangling each other with alarming regularity.

It was in this garden of understanding that I stopped to smell the lovely bouquet of Sincerity. (If you didn't say that was the worst line of narrative you have ever read, you haven't gotten into the spirit of Sincerity yet.) But if you look at Ben's precept for the week, you'll notice that he doesn't advocate complete honesty.

"Use no hurtful deceit; think innocently and justly, and if you speak, speak accordingly."

No hurtful deceit. Isn't that the key? Be completely honest? Always tell the absolute truth? Well, I would never want to advocate lying, but to suggest that absolute truth is desirable would be a tad naive (and possibly dangerous). Instead, it seems to me that what we are trying to avoid is deceit in its real form.

In trying to help me get a grasp on Franklin's meaning, Chris suggested that Franklin was an optimist. By asking us to avoid hurtful and deceptive thoughts and to think innocently of the world, he was suggesting that we use the power of our words to shape it into a wholesome, honest realm, uncorrupted by negativity.

Indeed, Chris suggested I go forward with three tenets for the week: optimism, a positive alternative, and a penchant for thinking innocently about the world. I could do that. If Franklin was an optimist, then that is just one more reason to admire him. I might not be able to discover electricity, but I can avoid hurtful deceit.

I just hope no one asks me how her dress looks.

A Day of Rest

Physician, heal thyself! In the previously mentioned spirit of Sincerity, I started the week by being honest with myself. I hate to admit personal weakness (though it may be painfully obvious to others), and therefore I rarely take a vacation. I don't need vacations, I tell myself. Vacations are for weaklings. I am not a weakling. On the first day of Sincerity, however, I admitted fatigue. I was tired. I was pooped from trying to be morally perfect. I needed a break, and I admitted that to myself (okay, now I'm starting to sound a little bit like a clinical psychologist or a guest on Oprah).

In keeping with this theme of honesty, aren't we all a little, well, driven? Don't we mistake effort for progress? A little time to stop and smell the flowers might not kill us; indeed, it might make us all the more virtuous.

Thus, I decided to take a "mental health" day. I would do nothing useful (so much for Industry), be of no help to anyone, and basically just enjoy my day. No helping with the kids, no housework. No projects so long neglected that Michelle has forgotten that she proposed them. No, this was to be a day of the completely useless. Following so closely on the heels of Industry, it had a delightfully anarchistic feeling.

Of course, doing nothing takes some effort.

Staying home and putting my feet up was not an option. Sooner rather than later some unfinished business would call to me. I expected it would come in the guilt-inducing voice of my wife. "If you're just going to sit there, maybe you could take five minutes to fix the toilet that's been running for two years."

She'd have been right, of course. There were many things I could have been doing, but the honest point of the day was to take a break. I needed to work at not working.

After helping get my children off to school, I left on my regular bus. I wasn't going anywhere, mind you. The idea was not to end up at any particular destination. If I had started to think about where to go, my unconscious mind would take me somewhere to do something. I wanted no *somethings*, so I needed to go nowhere—or at least nowhere I had planned.

It struck me as I exchanged small talk with my fellow travelers (most of whom seemed mildly concerned that I wasn't in a suit and tie) that I knew where to go.

I live in a suburb on the eastern extremes of the city. I knew from a glance at a transit map that my regular bus, after dropping me off in the city center, then traveled to the western suburbs. Where, specifically, I had no idea. I've often joked to my bus mates (a group of acquaintances who share little more in common than a neighborhood and a friendly rapport in the rear seats of our aging bus) that we should skip work, stay on the bus, and see where it takes us. We all laugh, take a deep breath, and head off to the daily grind. Worker bees heading back to the hive. On Day 1 of Sincerity, however, it wasn't a joke. On my sincere day off, I decided to see where the bus went.

"I'm doing it today," I announced. "I'm seeing where this bus goes." The reactions ranged from uninterested to mildly alarmed. Good to my word, I stayed on the bus as, one by one, my bus mates trudged off to another day of whatever it was they did all day. "Good luck," said one man as he got off at his stop, as if I were heading off into the Outback with no guide. In hindsight, there may have been a touch of sarcasm in his voice. "Tell us where it goes," said another. Maybe another touch of sarcasm.

As more and more stops passed, however, and I remained on the bus, a certain level of envy seemed to be developing among my fellow travelers. Like wishing someone off at the airport, there was a sense of *"I wish I were going, too"* among the regulars. It would not have been entirely surprising if someone threw down his or her briefcase and said, "The heck with work! I'm coming, too."

Okay, in the spirit of Sincerity, that would have been a total surprise and a little creepy. I was just riding to the end of a bus line, not flying to Casablanca on a whim.

Eventually, only the bus driver and I remained. At that point, a minor flaw in my hastily conceived plan emerged. My refusal to disembark appeared to make the driver nervous. As we drove farther and farther toward the opposite end of the city, I could see him examining me in his rearview mirror, concern creasing his brow. Indeed, he seemed on the verge of pulling the bus over to the side of the road and making a break for it. Clearly no one had ever taken a bus out of downtown at this time of the morning. "Fear not, good sir," I longed to say, "I am but a traveler on the bus to virtue." I decided that wouldn't quell his fears.

Fortunately, the extreme end of the run was only about a fifteen-minute ride. As we started our loop back through the western suburbs, picking up passengers at various stops, the driver relaxed in the presence of other commuters. When I finally rang the bell for a stop and disembarked back near the city center, he eyed me suspiciously.

{ *Trickery and treachery are the practices of fools that have not the wits enough to be honest.* }

The rest of the day was exactly what I had intended it to be: a day of "nothing." A Seinfeldian celebration of antiachievement. I wandered, I ate, I wandered some more. I sat on benches and watched the world go by. Nothing industrious was accomplished. I did no "good," I was not frugal. I was decidedly nonvirtuous . . . except I had been sincere. I needed a break, and I took it. Nothing was what I had needed, and nothing was what I had done. My personal honesty had been rewarded.

I should have explained all that to the bus driver. I really think I scared him.

Karma Takes a Hand

Sincerity is a strange beast. Most people would like to believe, I think, that they are honest. They value their reputations, their good names, and their ability to be trusted. And yet, we lie. Possibly we are not creatures of integrity but creatures of opportunity. It is said that there is no profit in lying. But what if there were? What if our jobs, our careers, our fortunes, or our lifestyles were at stake? What if our "profit" were the absence of losing something critical to us? Would we be likely to be truthful? Perhaps the best test of someone's integrity is when the jar holds the most cookies.

I got a chance to both see someone be tested and be tested myself in the week of Sincerity, thanks to the trial of an (alleged) impaired driver and a grandmother.

The trial was a run-of-the-mill impaired-driving trial, and notwithstanding an inevitable constitutional challenge, some scanty evidence on essential points, and a consistently well-prepared defense lawyer on the other side, I went into the trial with some (largely unwarranted) confidence. What I didn't know was that my main witness and the principal investigator differed, though neither of them knew it, on a central point of the evidence.

Here was Ben calling me out. In my pretrial interview of the main witness, an impossibly honest, hardworking man, it became apparent that though his testimony was going to provide most of the evidence against the accused, it was clearly going to strengthen the constitutional argument I was sure the defense was going to raise.

One of the obligations of a prosecutor is to reveal all of the relevant information in the hands of the prosecution to the accused. What the witness had told me was not really new. The rules of disclosure, looked at in a certain way, would not have required me to reveal what I had learned in the pretrial interview. Legal ambiguity aside, there was no way that I was going to hide the information from the defense. Even if my own personal moral code did not compel me to reveal it (which it did), my own sense of long-term career survival assured its revelation.

As I suspected, the lawyer used what I passed on from the witness. It strengthened the defense's case, and as a result of that and an error in some documents prepared by another witness, the charges were dismissed. Sincerity had taken a sizable bite out of my metaphorical derriere. Still, I knew I had done the right thing.

I'd like to give Ben Franklin all the credit for this little lesson in virtue. Unfortunately for the premise of this book, the real lesson had come from a grandmother and her troubled grandson.

Earlier in the day, before the unsuccessful prosecution of the impaired driver, I received a call from a woman who had been victimized by her grandson. She wanted me to know that over the weekend, her grandson had tried to take his own life with the assistance of his biological mother (yes, you read that right), who had provided him with a handful of pills. The grandmother, in the face of this colossal human tragedy, was depressed, frightened, and lost. She was watching her grandson, whom she had raised as her own, spiraling into a life of despair. She wasn't really seeking information or asking me to do anything. She was just letting me know that she had nowhere else to turn.

Later that day, during the sentencing of the young man, that same grandmother read her victim impact statement—a process that allows a victim to describe how a particular offender has affected his or her life. It was the epitome of Sincerity. The grandmother, often turning her attention directly to her grandson, told the court how much the financial burden of the theft was going to hurt her. What was worse, she explained, was the emotional burden of being betrayed. When it was the grandson's turn to speak—he had refused to be represented by legal aid—I saw another view of Sincerity. Cynical though I have become, it was difficult not to be moved as this young man cried, apologized to his grandmother, and confirmed her report that he had tried to take his own life the week before. His medication was not working, and he had nowhere to go.

As the judge struggled with what to do, the grandmother, who twenty minutes before wanted no contact with this man who had betrayed her trust, agreed to trust him again. She offered to let him live in her house. As I leaned back and conferred with her, concerned about why she was changing her mind, her answer was simple: "He has nowhere else to go." When we took a brief adjournment to see what other arrangements could be made, the young man looked at me, honest desperation in his eyes, and said, "I just want to go home so my grandmother can watch me."

{ *Honesty is the best policy.* }

Later, when my own personal test came, the answer to my dilemma was simple. I turned over the evidence, and the charges were dismissed. An old woman with more problems than I could imagine had shown me the way to virtue. Are we honest only when it is profitable? Can we be honest when it costs us? That is the Sincerity that Franklin demanded.

Making the "How Do I Look in This Dress?" Question Seem Simple

Early in his autobiography, Franklin tells a story about how, in his youth, he and some friends stole some stones intended for house construction to build a wharf from which he could fish. In the morning, the men working on the house discovered their loss of building material. Of what came next, Franklin wrote:

> Inquiry was made after the removers; we were discovered and complained of; several of us were corrected by our fathers; and though I pleaded the usefulness of the work, mine convinced me that nothing was useful which was not honest.

I suspect that Franklin's father's method of instruction was decidedly old school. Undoubtedly, however, the lesson was well
learned: "Nothing was useful which was not honest." On the other
hand, Albert Camus said: "How can sincerity be a condition of
friendship? A taste for truth at any cost is a passion which spares
nothing."

Where is the truth in this search for truth? Is there a balance
between the socially acceptable "little white lie" and the brutal honesty that repelled Camus?

I'm not sure if there is, but the need for balance in Sincerity was
tested by the most daunting of challenges. A request by my wife to
tell her what I thought of her.

Let me begin by saying that I love my wife. We have been together now close to two decades and have survived life's journey
with an equal measure of respect, humor, and affection. We have
survived, as a couple, despite the challenges of being the parents of
a special needs child, losing another child at birth, and all of the
other various and sundry crap that hits life's fan. That is not to say
that our marriage has been complete and unending bliss. Anyone
who makes this claim is not going to win any awards for Sincerity.
We have, however, made a good life together—a good life that could
not possibly be made better by her asking me what I think of her.
Of course, the irony of the situation is not lost on me. I had asked
Michelle the very same question at the beginning of my Franklin
experiment.

As we sat in the living room of our home, children tucked snugly
in their beds, my wife turned to me and said, "Some days I feel like
I'm a failure. I feel like I'm not doing enough. I'm trying to be a
good mother, good at my job, and a good wife, and some days it just
feels like I'm not good at any of them. Am I a failure?"

So why had Michelle asked me if she was a failure? Was she planning her own Franklinian quest? Why is it even important to know why she was asking? If this is a week of Sincerity, shouldn't Sincerity be the order of the day? Dare I answer "sloth" when she asks what type of animal she is?

Let me tell you why it is important and why such a question might be an occasion for a nuanced answer.

A question from one's spouse is filled with the context of the entire relationship. The answer given must likewise be colored by that context. A harsh word spoken ten years before, a forgotten anniversary, a chance meeting with a former girlfriend—any of these things and a hundred others may form the background or even the rationale for the question and must be anticipated in the answer. There is simply no way that the human mind, at least the 10 percent of it we use, can take into account all the possibilities. Thus, there can be no right answer. Honesty, in these circumstances, is a myth and, on a practical level, potentially dangerous.

And yet in the throes of the conclusion of the virtue of Sincerity, I was confronted with a question that called for this textured honesty. From the standpoint of the chronicler, this was an unbelievable opportunity—manna from heaven for the virtue seeker.

A big pile of sidewalk dog poo for a husband.

But whatever it meant to me, my wife's question meant so much more to her. She was seeking a real, honest assessment for her own reasons. She deserved Sincerity. You see, I knew, when my wife asked me what I thought of her, that she asked it in the context of her ongoing internal struggle over whether or not she had made the right choice to forgo her career—at least temporarily—to stay home with our three young children (she was just returning to work on a part-time basis). It is a classic struggle manifested by the nature of our modern society, one made all the more poignant for my wife by the fact that we are the parents of a child who requires special attention. That was, I understood, the context of my wife's question.

In that moment, I felt like a veil was lifted. For the first time in Ben Franklin's course, I understand a virtue completely, and that understanding had given me instant results. Sincerity, in the Franklin sense, provided a context for the answer my wife was seeking.

So I told my wife the truth. I told her that I think she is an extraordinary person, strong-willed, opinionated, and an excellent mother. I told her that I think she would be remembered by her children as a mother who made a sacrifice so that they could be happier. I told her that I believe in the fullness of time that she will regard this as a right decision regardless of what our children think. I told her the truth.

No "Do you like my dress?" questions and answers here. No textured truth. No Albert Camus. Just Sincerity, in the way I believe Franklin intended it.

I noted, for the first time, a clean slate on my virtue checklist.

I could have hugged Ben.

SINCERITY

	S	M	T	W	TH	F	SAT
USE NO HURTFUL DECEIT; THINK INNOCENTLY AND JUSTLY, AND IF YOU SPEAK, SPEAK ACCORDINGLY.							
Temperance		★	★	★		★	★★
Silence					★	★	★
Order	★	★	★★	★	★		
Resolution		★	★	★		★	
Frugality		★			★	★	
Industry	★		★		★		
Sincerity							
Justice					★		
Moderation		★				★	★
Cleanliness			★			★	
Tranquillity		★		★			★
Chastity							
Humility		★	★	★		★	★

CHAPTER 8

Justice

*Wrong none by doing injuries or omitting
the benefits that are your duty*

HERE'S A FACT ABOUT BENJAMIN FRANKLIN NOT WIDELY KNOWN. HE
was intensely proud of being an Englishman. And by Englishman,
I mean a citizen of England. That's what he considered himself: a
citizen of the land against which he would eventually take up arms
(metaphorically). Revolution would have been the last thing he
would have considered almost up to the point of . . . well . . . the
Revolution. He has been called a reluc-
tant revolutionary. He was an Englishman, was proud of it, and felt entitled
to the benefits that such citizenship en-
tailed. It is hard to think of Franklin as
a Loyalist nearly three centuries later, but that is exactly what he
was, at least up to the point where he believed that loyalty was no
longer warranted. Indeed, when he was the representative, in England, of several of the colonies, he had a notion that he might per-

{ *A countryman between
two lawyers is like a
fish between two cats.* }

manently relocate there. He enjoyed the rights and liberties of being an Englishman. It was only when he perceived that those rights were being unjustly withheld that he became one of the leaders of the creation of a new nation. How might the world have been different if King George and his boys had simply followed Franklin's course of virtues?

Though Franklin wrote of Justice long before the American Revolution, some of the reasons for his participation in that historic event can be found in this very virtue. Franklin understood Justice. I, on the other hand, was having another of my moments of self-doubt. Actually, they were adding up to hours at this point. Maybe weeks.

I am in the Justice business, of course, so one would think that this would have been a milestone for me on my way to moral perfection, a banner day on the road to virtue.

In fact, when I enlisted the help of my mentor, Chris, as a sort of expert guide in the land of ethics and morals, I suspected that this would be the one virtue in which I could give him a run for his intellectual money. (He's much smarter than me, you see. To be frank, most of the time I have trouble understanding what he's talking about.)

As usual, I was wrong.

It turns out that I was as lost about the notion of Justice (at least in the sense that Franklin meant it) as the average, non-Franklin-following citizen. I'm pretty sure that the Justice to which Franklin was referring had a far more personal, less throw-'em-in-jail quality than my type of Justice.

So what *was* Franklin's Justice? The answer lies, I believe, in what Edmund Morgan described as "the end of his pragmatism." After describing the essential practicality—the pragmatism—that seems to permeate our understanding of Franklin as "a willingness to compromise in pursuit of some goal," Morgan poses the question, "Where did Franklin's pragmatism end . . . ?"[1] In answering his own question, Morgan acknowledges that even during Franklin's pursuit of some of his most treasured goals, he remained prepared to be, well, pragmatic. There were instances, however, in which Franklin, refused to give in:

> But there were occasions when he dug in his heels and refused to make concessions, occasions when his goal was nonnegotiable, when defeat was preferable to compromise, when his pragmatism came to an end, a stop.[2]

So what were those "occasions"? Certainly, his fight for the rights of "Americans" and, even before that, his fight against the Penn family in their capacity as proprietors of Pennsylvania. The most compelling to modern sensibilities, however, might be his last fight—his last cause. Franklin made his last act of public service a plea to the first U.S. Congress to end slavery. While some have questioned his sincerity on the issue, it seems to me that in this position, this last act of a public servant, we see Franklin's sense of Justice. His petition to Congress said that "equal liberty was originally . . . the birthright of all men." These were the benefits that he saw as his duty, indeed the duty of his new country, to confer.

So that was the type of Justice that Franklin sought. It was a far more profound, foundational brand of Justice than what I had first envisioned when I examined the virtues. This virtue was going to be tougher than it first appeared.

Discovering My Justice Mantra

On the first day of Justice, Justice and Tranquillity met at a crossroads and tried to beat each other senseless.

I had spent the better part of the day in a trial with a lawyer whose questioning style can best be described as glacial. What would normally take minutes takes hours, hours become days, and days turn into weeks. This is not good. Like milk, Justice gets smelly if it stays around too long.

But in the spirit of Franklin, I was trying to take a broad view of Justice. Perhaps my opponent on this day understood that too often in the criminal justice system, we settle for expediency when the goal should be truth. Maybe, in fact, my desire, at that moment, to strangle him was a reflection of my own poor character and lack of a holistic view of Justice rather than a reaction to his annoying courtroom style.

As I sat, head in hands, listening to the endless drone of his voice, lamenting the bad luck that assigned me to this court on this day, I realized that this was a Franklinian catch-22.

My obligation to participate in this process, to see that Justice was done, was running headlong into my inability, at the moment, to be tranquil. Justice required a fair trial, and my opponent seemed to have the view that a fair trial required him to ask the same questions of witnesses over and over and over again. In this regard, then, Justice was being served (sort of).

My adversary, as pedantic as he might have been, brought home to me that I might simply be a cog in a massive wheel rather than Justice Man. The system functions, as I've earlier described, a little like an airline that overbooks seats. Airlines hope that not everyone who books passage shows up wanting to fly somewhere. Courts are like that. More trials are scheduled than can be logically dealt with, not enough time is assigned to any event on the docket, and when someone is told to do or not do something as part of the consequence for his or her crime, there is little or no follow-up. To continue the airline analogy, when everyone demands their day in court, the plane can't fly. There are just not enough seats.

Some days I feel like the system provides excellent value to society. On other days, I feel like a factory worker on the assembly line, putting my one small part onto the big car of Justice—nothing handmade about this baby.

So if my opponent felt it was his duty, his requirement, to do Justice, to ask the same questions repeatedly, then my obligation was to make sure they were asked properly and that our little notion of Justice was fulfilled. At least I think that's what I thought. It is all something of a blur now. My concentration was lost in the endless droning from my adversary.

As much as Justice, in the best Benjamin Franklin tradition, might have been present in that courtroom, Tranquillity had thrown its things into a suitcase and had run away as fast as its little legs could carry it.

Maybe I need a mantra.

I will not strangle other lawyers. I will not strangle other lawyers.

I Fought Irony, and Irony Won

Justice and irony must be first cousins. They both have a way of sneaking up on you. Just when you think you have the whole notion of fulfilling your responsibilities to others down, Justice walks up behind you, slaps you across the back of the head, and scolds you for letting everyone down.

{ *Without justice courage is weak.* }

You may remember my pro bono project from an earlier chapter. Well, Justice seemed just the week to dedicate to this endeavor. For an instant, I thought that my dedication to this Justice-based initiative might even have found favor with Franklin himself, for in the middle of the week of Justice I had a metaphorical victory for my efforts.

The catalyst for the idea had been a couple who had been wronged by a government agency. They came to me for help, but given what I do for a living, there was little that I could do for them. I did the best I could, making several recommendations about not-for-profit organizations that might be of some assistance, all the while knowing that these were Band-Aid solutions. Thus, I formulated the idea for our Pro Bono Association.

As I said, in the middle of the week dedicated to Justice, I saw some cosmic hand at work. I was working late in my office again when I ran into the couple who had been my inspiration. They were excited to see me. The husband told me that one of my suggestions had helped and, in the end, saved him $4,000.

As I congratulated him, I thought of Ben and his dictate not to omit our duties and was pleased with the symbolic victory in a week dedicated to Justice.

I should have known that Benjamin Franklin would have scorned symbolic victories. The next day, there were to be no victories, symbolic or otherwise.

Let me begin my tale of Justice woe by giving you a little background. My boss had been away for three weeks. In an office of six prosecutors, the loss of one can cause significant workload strains. One of my colleagues was also out on extended sick leave. Meanwhile, I was under a looming deadline to prepare a legal brief in response to an appeal of a murder conviction. Heaped on that were the regular files, a number of deadlines for filings of documents in future trials, and several requests for advice from law enforcement agencies.

That would have been a busy, if typical, week. But in that week of Justice, nothing was to be typical. On top of all the regular work, I had agreed to assist a prosecutor in a neighboring jurisdiction with the upcoming trial of a brutal double homicide. While this was the work I had dreamed of when I was in law school (as much as I have ever dreamed of work), it also added considerably to my caseload.

Despite the fact that this trial had all the ingredients of a Hollywood movie, the real story was less dramatic yet far more compelling. The family of a murder victim can never be restored to normalcy. They can't be put back in the position in which they were before the crime. Part of my job, I think, was to prepare them for what lay ahead.

And here is where my hubris at the symbolic victory of the previous day met up in a dark alley with irony. My hubris took a tremendous beating.

The accused in the murder trial, a man who had apparent mental health problems, was returning from a psychiatric exam. The appearance in court was to last no more than a few minutes. A report would be filed and a date set for a hearing on the issue of his fitness to stand trial. Not much for me to do (given that I was what is referred to as "second chair"—kind of Robin to the other prosecutor's Batman). That was what I had told myself. But I forgot about Justice. I omitted to confer the benefits that were my duty.

One of my jobs, in a system that is complex, overburdened, and confusing, is to be a guide. I should have explained, directed, and managed expectations. I should have prepared the family for what could *possibly* occur, not what probably would occur. I had led the family to believe that this would be a quick appearance—an "in and out."

Instead it was a circus.

The accused used this quick appearance to put on a show. Real or contrived, he went on a rant. He tried, unsuccessfully, to fire his lawyer, he taunted the victim's family, and he rambled at the judge.

Of course, I didn't know that any of this was going to happen, but I should have known it might. And knowing this, I should have told the family. It would not have changed anything, but at least they would have been forewarned. It was a benefit owed to them, a duty imposed on me. I denied them their benefit and, thus, in the Franklinian sense, did an injustice. It was not even something of which I could make light.

Oh, that the day could have ended there.

As soon as the supposedly short appearance was over, I had to rush to a different courtroom. The circumstance was far less gruesome, the loss less significant. A man with his own emotional issues, and a growing propensity to defraud local businesses, had swindled a hardware store out of several thousand dollars in merchandise. The accused was to have gone to trial on this day but had obtained the services of a legal-aid lawyer. The lawyer was certain, after a brief perusal of the file, that his new client would be pleading guilty but needed more time. Knowing the length of the day's docket, the likelihood that the judge involved would grant an adjournment whatever my position, and the likelihood of an eventual guilty plea, I agreed to the lawyer's request. The only thing remaining was to explain what had happened to the business owner and his employees.

My explanation was anything but satisfactory. As I listened to a mild harangue from the business owner about delays and his general lack of faith in the justice system, I was quite certain that I had been a major disappointment to Ben Franklin on this day. I had slipped in the other virtues; my chart was full of transgressions. This, however, was the first time that the failures meant more than something about which to write. This was a real virtuous malfunction.

As I continued to subject myself to an earful from the business owner, I tried to look on the bright side. At least I was getting to hear what the victim thought about Justice.

Old Knees but Young Hearts

Call this an ode to faded glory or a song for fleeting youth.

{ *He that won't be*
counseled can't be
helped.}
On the weekend of the week dedicated to Justice, I took part in one of
the oldest rituals known to man: a
gathering of ancient warriors to test
their prowess and relive the days when
their arms were strong, their legs swift, and their cares few. The
battleground for these heroes of yesterday was a thirty-five-and-over
basketball tournament. My team, which had recently lost in the fi-
nals of the thirty-five-and-over city league, reunited to take on the
best of the rest of the province in their age category for a chance at
immortality—"B" division.

As I packed my gym bag and clothes after work on Friday night,
I had my usual qualms about going away for a weekend. A young
family calls for the presence of its parents, children need the attention of their father, and I have always had a reasonable level of guilt
whenever I abandon that responsibility for even the shortest times.
Going away for a weekend to play in a basketball tournament with
other slightly overweight, creaky-kneed, graying, former athletes
seemed an indulgence. There was also the cost. I knew that my beer
and pizza bill was going to be substantially larger on this weekend.

In truth, I would probably not have gone to the weekend
tournament had my mother not encouraged me. Earlier, when I
told her that I was unlikely to attend, she said, "Oh, go. Everyone
needs a break." Her birthday present money to me was the registra-
tion fee.

The tournament was being held in a city an hour and a half
away from my home, and so my team—a university professor, two
IT executives, a grocer, a biologist, a salesman, an educator, and a

prosecutor (all of whose knees and fitness had seen better days—crammed our gym bags into our cars and took a road trip. We converged on the site of our first game—lose and end up in the consolation round; win and our hope for glory remained. Forty minutes later, we knew the elation of advancing to the next level (and the anxiety of overtaxing our cardiovascular systems). A trip to a local pub for a celebratory drink, a game of pool, and a late-night pizza and I felt the cares of the week passing away.

I shouldn't really have been surprised that I was having a good time. I love basketball—any team sport really—and I loved being part of a team again. Maybe it's the pack mentality of humans or some latent martial instinct that man never escapes, but team sports hold a special place in most men's hearts (I know I am being sexist, but indulge me for a moment)—no matter how bad the team. And it had been a good year. Our team's personalities jelled, we played well in our league, and we usually enjoyed some postgame socializing with some of the other league teams.

After our Saturday game, another victory—this time over one of our city league opponents who also made the trip to the tournament—there was a social at a private club. After the meal, as I sat watching some of my teammates hold a pool table against all comers, I marveled at the effect of our short return to the games of boyhood. Grown men, men burdened and blessed with the responsibilities of adulthood, acted like the children they had once been. The jokes were juvenile, the razzing unrelenting, and the competition friendly (for the most part). A sort of euphoria had come over most of us, temporary though it might have been. I could see real joy in the faces of people whose brow wrinkles revealed the effects of age and worry, and I wondered why it is that we lose the joy of youth so easily. Why do we, as adults, deprive ourselves of the fun, camaraderie, and sometimes plain silliness that mark our early years? Maybe if we remembered, and lived, a little more like kids, then the burden of responsibility wouldn't seem so heavy.

On Sunday, our final game—the Masters "B" Division Basketball Championship—was played in front of a fluctuating but enthusiastic crowd of between four and ten. Despite an early setback, our team rallied, played as stifling a defense as thirty- to forty-five-year-old knees would allow, and emerged as champions. You would think by the high-fives, embraces, expressions of pure joy when the medals were presented, and postgame locker room toast that we had won a tournament for the ages rather then a tournament of the aged. We'd be lucky to garner a one-inch mention in the local paper.

But it wasn't glory that we were seeking, that kind of glory we all know is in our past (at least as far as sports go). We knew that our real success was in showing up and remembering that we were once kids who ran and jumped and played. Real success was in not just remembering the past but knowing that the future can include still being those kids, if for only part of the time, and never really growing up—not completely. Winning was just icing on the cake. I gave my medals (we asked for extras for those of us with more than one child at home) to my girls—they took them to school the next day to show their friends that their dad was a champion. The looks on their faces when I handed them the medals reminded me that there is glory in being an adult as well. Maybe the secret is in finding the balance.

What, you may be asking yourself, does all this have to do with Franklin's course of virtues, and particularly Justice? I wondered that myself as I sat in the poolroom listening to my teammates razz me about my inability to knock them off the table. It was then that I realized the real lesson of the week. Citizen Ben warned himself, and by extension those who follow, to do Justice by not *omitting the benefits that are your duty.* I thought when I first started the week that this virtue was all about doing right by others. As I watched my friends, and felt the real joy in my heart at this gathering, I realized that being virtuous, doing Justice, not omitting the benefits that were my duty, referred not just to others but to me as well.

As my mother said, "Everybody needs a break." If we are to be virtuous, we need to do virtue to ourselves, to ensure that we remember those things that are the best of ourselves and embrace them and enjoy life. Franklin knew this and knew that in seeking moments of happiness for himself, in not omitting the benefits he owed to himself, he was better able to do Justice to others.

I realize this all might sound like some after-the-fact justification for a weekend away, eating pizza and drinking beer. My attempt to persuade myself that this road trip was somehow related to Justice is perhaps just a self-deceiving rationalization.

Oh well, at least this wasn't the week of Sincerity.

JUSTICE

WRONG NONE BY DOING INJURIES OR OMITTING THE BENEFITS THAT ARE YOUR DUTY.							
	S	M	T	W	Th	F	Sat
Temperance		★	★		★★	★★	★
Silence	★	★			★		
Order			★★		★		
Resolution		★				★	★
Frugality	★				★	★★	★
Industry		★					
Sincerity	★				★		
Justice			★	★		★	
Moderation				★			
Cleanliness		★					★
Tranquillity		★★	★★★				
Chastity							
Humility	★	★★	★			★	★

CHAPTER 9

Moderation

*Avoid extremes; forbear resenting injuries
so much as you think they deserve*

UP UNTIL MODERATION, MY FAILURES ALONG THE PATH OF VIRTUE HAD
been modest (as have been my successes). I might not have been
lighting the virtuous world afire, but nor was I in danger of
being stoned to death by some Ben Franklin cult. At least until
Moderation.

{ *When in doubt, don't.* }

Moderation threatened me with a
heretofore forgotten foe: mediocrity. For once (just once, mind
you), I thought I had too much of what Ben sought (or at least
some boring mutation of what he sought). There was a successful
song from the 1940s called "Accentuate the Positive." You know
it—catchy tune, interesting little lyrics. The refrain is "Don't mess
with Mr. In-Between." Well, don't mess with me. I am Mr. In-
Between.

I am the epitome of Moderation. For the most part, my life has
been governed by very middle-of-the-road behavior. I certainly didn't

set out to be moderate; in fact, I probably expected to be a creature of extremes—extremely successful, extremely happy, extremely
everything. The reality is that I am only extremely moderate.

In hindsight, I think my Moderation became a self-fulfilling
prophecy. As I navigated my way through moderate successes, I
avoided risk for fear of losing the benefits of the moderate success,
thereby assuring my Moderation. When Chris and I talked about
the week of Moderation, he railed against such careful mediocrity.
"Moderation is preached as a virtue precisely because it shuts down
revolt and stifles innovation. It reinforces the status quo and casts
doubts on those who question the way things 'have always been,'"
he said. Indeed, this was the most animated he had been about any
virtue. This one seemed to stick in his craw. Of course, he had not
been moderate in his life. He had traveled the world and lived in
other countries. He speaks several languages and embraces cultures
other than his own. He is not Mr. In-Between.

I understood and appreciated his rant (though I should have
encouraged him to tone it down just a little bit—no need to go to
extremes). Somewhere inside me, there is an extremist yelling and
protesting against the innate conservatism of my existence. Stop
being Mr. Cleaver, I tell myself. Jump out of airplanes, go heli-skiing,
race cars. But I do none of these things. Instead, I am careful. I walk
down the center of the road (ensuring that the road has previously
been closed for my safety), find the balance in all things. Even on
those occasions when I seek to cast off the chains of my Moderation,
I usually just trip over them.

When I was graduating from college, I decided I needed to experience the world outside North America. My university had a
small library dedicated specifically to this type of wanderlust. Would
it be teaching English in Korea or tutoring in Japan? Maybe I could
do some sort of charity work in Africa. The more I researched, the

more my moderate self protested, "Whoa, big fella! Let's not wander too far out of the yard. It's a dangerous world out there. How about a weekend in the city?"

Finally, I rejected all notions of altruism and decided on a backpacking trip through Europe. I even convinced my cousin to go with me. It was more moderate than my first notions of my postgraduate activities, yet it still had a sense of adventure for me. I scrimped and saved, divested myself of all worldly possessions, and readied myself for my European escapade. I was heading out into the big, bad world. Moderation be damned.

On the first night of the trip, not long after stepping off the plane in Brussels, my backpack was stolen from a locker room in our hostel. "Told you so," said my inner moderate.

My reaction to this Day 1 theft was to hop on a train and flee Belgium. Actually, not just Belgium but all of Continental Europe. My cousin and I didn't stop until we had passed through France, crossed a small portion of the Atlantic and all of the Celtic Sea. We didn't take a breath until we hit Ireland. I think I chose Ireland because it was more familiar. There is enough Irish in me that after my misadventure in Brussels, Dublin seemed almost like home.

Of course, the cost of replacing my stolen clothes meant that my trip money was dwindling faster than I had expected (and replacing clothes for a six-foot-three man in Ireland proved more difficult than I'd expected; the Irish, from whom I am in part descended, are evidently a vertically challenged people). The whole debacle dramatically shortened my time in Europe. Indeed, it would turn the backpacking adventure into an extended vacation. My six-month trip turned into less than six weeks.

I've always blamed the early termination of the trip on the cost of buying new clothes, but in truth, it was just a manifestation of a middle-of-the-road personality. An unscripted free-flowing journey across unknown countries was too much for me—too extreme. A nice, long vacation was far more acceptable. It was moderate.

So for me, Moderation should have been just another day. At least I should have had no trouble with the acquisition of this virtue.

But as I approached this, the ninth virtue, I knew that this milquetoast, overly safe vision of Moderation was not what Franklin had in mind. Ben was not Mr. In-Between.

Ben took risks. Ben did things. Ben changed the world. He gambled and was rewarded. These are not the actions of a moderate in any sense of the word. So what did Franklin mean when he instructed himself to be moderate?

Alan Houston explains Franklin's Moderation as part of his self-created scheme, five decades in the making, of winning people over to his side of any issue. According to Houston, it was simply a form of politeness:

> Politeness was the virtue of a sensible man. Franklin's extraordinary success in politics can be attributed, in no small measure, to his embodiment of this early-eighteenth-century ideal.[1]

For Ben, Moderation, like politeness, was a method to personal gain. Don't aggravate anyone too much. Don't make too many waves. Steer the middle course in the waters of social contact. I'm not sure that it is the most altruistic of Ben's virtues, but judging by his achievements, it served him well.

Not everyone appreciated it. Again according to Houston, John Adams described Franklin's Moderation (having seen it in action in France and having himself failed at a more extreme tact) as an affront to good manners and decency. Thomas Jefferson, on the other hand, having the same advantage of observation, recognized Franklin's amiability as a method of persuasion. In the end, the French loved Ben and hated John Adams.[2]

Regardless of Franklin's view of this virtue as a method of persuasion, it is at least more striving than my style of Moderation.

So how, then, could I achieve Ben's virtue this week? Ben's autobiography holds a key. Franklin described how over time he modified the way he engaged in discourse. First, recognizing a tendency to argue for argument's sake (and the inherent dangers of that tendency), he, upon discovering Socrates, took up the ancient philosopher's method of persuasion. It worked well, to a point. Though he was able to use it to trap others into concessions, he was, at the same time, losing their favor. Thus, he resolved to further modify his style of conversation and developed a habit that he described as a great advantage to him. He adopted a temperament of "modest diffidence," whereby he avoided words "that give the air of positiveness to an opinion." Rather he would say, "I conceive or apprehend a thing to be so and so; it appears to me, or I should think it so or so, for such and such reasons; or I imagine it to be so; or it is so, if I am not mistaken."

Essentially, as it appears to me (see I've learned a thing or two), Franklin had adopted the position of never taking a position. In debate or conversation, he became a centrist. Avoid the extremes and hug the middle of the road. Maybe he was Mr. In-Between.

Well, that was a style of Moderation that might prove useful. I have a habit of arguing for sport. As momentarily engaging as debate may be, it does seem to have the distinct disadvantage of annoying people. Thus, in my week of Moderation, I resolved to try to be moderate in my positions, diffident in my expressions, and unassuming in my arguments. It had potential. I could see myself, confronted with some statement of monumental ignorance, biting back a caustic slur and instead asking, "That's interesting. How did you come to that conclusion?"

Sounds kind of smarmy, I thought, when I said it like that. Oh well, I had a week to work on it.

I was not letting myself off the hook on the other aspect of Moderation. Chris Levan had thrown down a gauntlet against my style of Moderation and cried for a little Dylan Thomasesque railing against the dying of the light. Interestingly, this virtue came on the week in which I was to celebrate my thirty-ninth birthday (more on this later). How ironic that a virtue I may have mastered to the point of stagnation arose in the middle of my life (the last time I checked, the life expectancy of a male in my locale was somewhere in the vicinity of seventy-eight—that made me quite literally middle-aged). Perhaps this was more than irony; maybe this was the subtle hand of fate (guided by Ben and Chris) pushing me to evaluate more than a particular virtue. Was I being goaded into evaluating an entire life? Had my middle-of-the-road choices been the right ones? Had my Moderation served me well? Should I have been a risk taker?

{ *He that composes himself is wiser than he that composes a book.*}

Two roads in the woods diverged, and I took the one clearly marked on the visitor's map.

So as I followed Ben to Moderation, I would simultaneously race away from it. I was destined to meet myself somewhere in the middle. At least I'd be walking at a safe pace.

Modest Diffidence . . . Whatever That Is

I tried, on the first day of the week, to develop some plan for how I would approach the method of moderate conversation that marks Franklin's virtue. I didn't anticipate much success, and I was right.

Imagine going through a day trying to be diffident in your positions. Appreciate, if you can, that this requires you to nod, offer some level of empathetic understanding, and not clearly contradict every stupid, inane, ridiculous proposition put to you by . . . well . . . everyone. There are a lot of people whose opinions demand a belligerent, antagonistic, brash response—a sort of rhetorical beat down. Ben's method does not allow for this.

After only a few hours of trying this never-take-a-position business, I wanted to tell Ben what I thought of his method of speech.

I resolved, however, to put aside my misgivings and give Franklin's Moderation a try. I will not, I told myself, under any circumstances, express certainty about any position. Indeed, I would not make it apparent to anyone that I had adopted a position at all. Assuming I had . . . adopted a position, that is . . . which I had not. At least not one that I will share with you.

Maybe I had better review Franklin's Moderation again. He expressed his Moderation as a method of conversation in which he would eschew words such as "certainly" or "without question" or any other expressions of conviction. Rather he would say:

> I conceive or apprehend a thing to be so and so; it appears to
> me, or I should think it so or so, for such and such reasons; or
> I imagine it to be so; or it is so, if I am not mistaken.

If I am not mistaken, I told myself, this is going to drive me nuts.

And so it did. As I went through the day practicing this, I experienced both guilt at being untruthful and an uncomfortable feeling of kinship with a former superior. The sense of guilt I can handle— I've done enough stupid things in my life that guilt is not an unknown emotion. This course by itself had engendered enough failure that I am almost immune to the effects of guilt and self-doubt.

On the other hand, the feeling of some similarity or association to this past "boss" (I use that word loosely, as he was not a direct superior but several levels of bosses above me) had me shuddering like an alcoholic with the DTs.

I value certain qualities in people: honesty, integrity, and selflessness, among others. In those who occupy positions of leadership, I also appreciate three things: (1) a sense of mission; (2) decisiveness; and (3) a Trumanesque acceptance of responsibility. I want a leader who knows where the buck should go; directs the buck with conviction; and, when the buck goes astray, knows precisely where the buck should stop.

The boss I feared that I resembled, as I attempted Moderation, was no buck stopper.

My clearest memories of him are the interminable meetings. Here is how the meetings would go. He'd state the issue at hand, this would take an inordinate amount of time and might or might not actually address the relevant issue, and in doing so he would use a method of discourse similar to Ben's. He would never take a particular position, but he would adopt an inquiring posture. He might have intended it to be Socratic, but he was no Socrates. Nothing ever developed of his questions. No wisdom was drawn out from his inquiries. I left whatever meetings I attended with him having no idea what had been decided.

I'm not bitter about this time in my life. What concerned me was that as I spoke to people in my best Franklinian manner, I sounded like that guy!

Here's an example. On Day 1 of Moderation, a police officer asked me for advice on a question of law. This happens all the time.

I'm flattered by their trust in me, and I am mindful of my obligation to provide sound advice. Unfortunately, that week, I was also burdened with trying to master Franklin. Thus, while he expected a clear, if not concise, answer, what the officer got was some garbled, nonsensical inquiry about what the officer knew about the topic. He looked at me as if I were crazy. I suspected he thought I knew nothing about the topic and was just trying to hide my ignorance with some verbal shell game.

I tried again—same result. Finally, I just told him the answer. As he thanked me, I sensed that he thought I was having some sort of breakdown.

Worse, perhaps, than my lack of success with Franklin's method of communication was my lack of success at hiding that I was trying to use Franklin's method of communication.

Near the end of the day, I stopped into a colleague's office. "Am I glad to see you. I need some advice on a file," she said.

"Shoot," I replied.

"Remember that sexual assault file we were talking about? Well, the defense lawyer has said his client will plead if we ask for less than two years. What do you think?"

What an opportunity! I could feel the gentle hand of Franklin guiding me toward a moderate approach. I had a view on the question—a strong view. Ben would tell me not to simply state that view. If I wanted my friend to accept my position, I needed to win her over by making it her position. I would do so by using the Franklin Moderation method. My plan started with a simple statement beginning with the words "it appears to me," or "if I am not mistaken." Eventually, I would have her adopting a point of view, my point of view, without ever telling her that it was my point of view.

Things did not go as planned.

{ *He that would live in
peace and at ease must
not speak all he knows
or all he sees.*}

"It appears to me as if you need to consider the positives and negatives of the deal," I said.

Maybe it was the manner in which I said it, or perhaps I had a smug look on my face, or maybe it was just the weight of her knowledge about what I had been doing over the past two months. Whatever the cause, as soon as I had said it, she replied, "That's the most inane, obvious thing I have ever heard. This has something to do with that stupid course of virtues, doesn't it. When will this Franklin thing be done?"

I was beginning to wonder that myself.

Do Not Go Gentle into That Good Night

I was taking a stand. On the week of Moderation, I decided to take up the standard that Chris has passed and I am riding forth. Franklin's entire course (but for this virtue) calls out for change, for challenge, for chance taking. Chris has preached against Moderation. I have acknowledged a surfeit of "middle-of-the-road" disease. Why then should this virtue be anything different?

For the last five years or so, I have taken my birthday off for the express purpose of trying new things. I try a new drink, I try a new restaurant, and ostensibly, I try a new activity. The reality is that my new activities are generally quite mundane. The first year of my birthday/adventure, I tried ten-pin bowling. As I *attacked* this new activity, I learned three things: (1) I wasn't a bad bowler; (2) the average age at a bowling alley at 11:00 a.m. is about sixty-eight; and (3) my idea of a new activity needed some reconsideration.

Unfortunately, it really hasn't gotten any better over the years. My "new" activities haven't progressed very far, adventure-wise. I haven't taken the opportunity to pull the rip cord, either literally or figuratively. Thus, Franklin's call to Moderation (and Chris's call away from it) is for me a call to arms.

After my difficult beginning with modest diffidence, I changed my goal for Moderation on the day of my birth. I would jump from that plane (figuratively—it is far too cold here in April to take up skydiving). My new activity needed to be something more than it had been in the past. (I took a self-guided tour of historic buildings last year. Even the sixty-eight-year-old bowling crowd would have fallen asleep on that one.) The problem, however, was what to do (a problem exacerbated by lack of another virtue, Order, as I had done no planning and was thinking about this the morning of my birthday).

Over the years I have considered the obvious ones: skydiving (rejected for already stated reasons and a fear that my bulk and gravity might conspire against any parachute harness); taking up an instrument (hardly a one-day activity); and a spontaneous trip out of town (can't slip that one past Michelle). Oh well; I'd figure something out, I told myself.

I didn't.

Figure something out, that is.

I should have considered my options in advance, done some research, made arrangements for something spectacular. I didn't. No airplanes, no car racing, no derring-do at all. Undoubtedly, my lack of splashy new activity was a product not just of my lack of planning but also of my Moderation. Had I thought about this in advance, had I done some planning, would I have done something irresponsible? Probably not. I would have thought of my children and how they needed a father, or I would have considered the fool-hardiness of making some expense for no purpose. I would have been moderate.

In the end, my adventure—my new activity—made bowling look positively extreme. I simply wandered around town looking for anything I had not done before (within acceptable risk limits). I went into a store I had never visited, ate at restaurants that I had previously shunned, and had a drink previously untested (just one, even though I was taking the bus). Hardly a blow struck for living life to the fullest.

Chris was disappointed. Ben, I suspect, would also view this as a failure. He would just put it in moderate terms.

There's always next year.

As long as I'm careful.

A Moderate Failure

I'm not sure if I failed miserably or succeeded completely. I had really done nothing for the week of Moderation.

Well, that's not true. I had been absolutely moderate. I lived my life the way that I live my life every week. I followed my daily routine to a tee, avoiding extremes and forbearing resenting injuries. I suppose, then, that I had been moderate. Moderation has been, as usual, my watchword.

Why, then, did I feel like a virtuous failure? Did Ben envision mediocrity as a goal?

Maybe. Maybe Franklin was simply putting a metaphorical brake on himself during his own virtuous journey.

Remember Ben was a believer in the common person. He believed in advancement by achievement. In *Benjamin Franklin: An American Life*, Walter Isaacson explains the difference between Franklin and Thomas Jefferson. Jefferson believed in a natural aristocracy, while Franklin believed in a meritocracy. He believed in what he called the "middling" people."[3] He believed in coming up from the ranks, so to speak. His founding of what would become the University of Pennsylvania was, in part, an attempt to elevate people from all walks of life who wanted to better themselves.[4]

Maybe all of the change that he was attempting to facilitate in his own course of virtue led to the occasional episode of disengagement. Rush ahead too far from the pack and realize that you are in the wilderness on your own. Maybe Franklin, by advocating Moderation, was just trying to stay within a reasonable distance of the pack—to keep company with his middling people.

Whatever Ben's motivations, I have been the epitome of Moderation. It hasn't been particularly fun. No bumps and twists this week, just predictability, mediocrity, and acquiescence.

It was safe, though, and no one got hurt.

I am Mr. In-Between.

Sigh.

MODERATION

	S	M	T	W	Th	F	Sat
AVOID EXTREMES; FORBEAR RESENTING INJURIES SO MUCH AS YOU THINK THEY DESERVE.							
Temperance		★	★	★	★		
Silence		★	★★				
Order			★	★	★		
Resolution		★					
Frugality							
Industry		★			★		
Sincerity					★		
Justice			★				
Moderation	★★★★		★★★				★★★★
Cleanliness		★		★			
Tranquillity		★★	★★★				
Chastity							
Humility		★★	★	★			

CHAPTER 10

Cleanliness

Tolerate no uncleanliness in body, clothes, or habitation

I ONCE LIVED IN A CLOSET.

I tell you this because you would think that Cleanliness would be the one virtue of Franklin's about which there could be no controversy, no question of its efficacy. Undoubtedly in eighteenth-century America, personal cleanliness remained an issue of some debate; in the world's great cities, unsanitary conditions led to disease and even social unrest. But we, the denizens of the developed world in the twenty-first-century, are über-clean. Too clean perhaps. According to some researchers, too much cleanliness is hindering the immune systems of people in wealthy countries.

{ *Clean your finger before you point at my spots.* }

Thus my closet story. It may help explain my low incidence of illness in college.

During my final year of my first degree, I had to complete a term of student teaching. I did this at a school near my hometown. That was good—I saved a term's worth of rent by living at home. Unfortunately, the student teaching term was in the fall semester; thus, after Christmas I had to return to college midway through a normal school year. That was bad—I had nowhere to live.

To my good fortune, I had nice friends. They let me move into their apartment at a greatly reduced rent. I would throw a mattress on the floor of one of the rooms and all would be well.

We forgot to factor in my snoring.

After the first night on the floor, my new roomie said, "This isn't going to work. You snore like a water buffalo."

Now I had a dilemma. I needed a place to stay, but I didn't want to inconvenience the very friends who had granted me shelter in my time of want. It was then that I noticed the closet.

The apartment, a two-bedroom on the bottom floor of an aging building, had a strange configuration. The design of the building meant that the closet in the front hallway was approximately three feet by six and a half feet deep. I considered my dilemma, thought of my snoring-averse friend and meager rent, and decided that this particular closet looked like a very small room. Miraculously, my single mattress fit perfectly. It was fate.

Truth be told, I can't remember how long I actually slept in the closet. I do remember upgrading to the couch at some point. The closet, however, remained, in essence, my room.

Living in a closet is a unique experience. There is a certain womblike comfort to being encased by walls, a sense of coziness. On the other hand, there is literally no way to roll out of bed. When I got up in the morning, I had to squirm down to the end of the mattress and more or less eject myself.

The closet was also a bit of a date killer. I'm not saying that I was trying to pick up girls and bring them home (not while my mother is alive to read this book), but even bringing a date back for dinner, a drink, or a movie all had to happen in the knowledge that they would almost certainly ask, "So which room is yours?"

The biggest problem, however, was the cleanliness. It is difficult to maintain even a college dorm room level of cleanliness in a closet. Hardly *Better Homes and Garden*.

As I have matured, so have my living quarters. From closet to apartment to marital apartment, I passed through the stages of life as I climbed the evolutionary ladder of Cleanliness. There remains, however, a certain amount of the closet dweller in me. There is still a little "closet" in my house.

I don't mean that my house is unclean, at least no more so than any house that shelters three young children; it's just that there seems to be a lot more *stuff* than there needs to be.

I did not view this as a reason for surrender. Rather, I embraced Cleanliness. Unlike Moderation, I believed that it offered the opportunity for a concrete change in my behavior. Perhaps it is my nature as a pragmatist. My need for concrete results may simply be a virtual hangover from the more abstract concepts of Moderation and Justice. Cleanliness was something I could sink my teeth into.

Indeed, for the first time in weeks, I had a concrete plan of action. Borrowing from my week of Order, I decided to attempt to enforce organization on my personal space. I would sift, sort, discard, gift, and otherwise divest myself of those items of clutter that had been with me longer than my children (note of clarification—I had no plans to discard my children).

There was, unfortunately, an enemy in the camp in this virtue—a spy for the forces of pack rats.

As you might recall from the chapter on Order, my mother refuses to discard things. She doesn't collect garbage; she just does not

believe in "out with the old, in with the new." In this age of overflowing landfills, she never seems to throw anything out. (I think it
is important for me to stop and note that my mother keeps a very
clean house; she is in no way *unclean*—she just keeps stuff). When
she reads this, she'll probably wonder why she kept me.

My parents' basement is filled with old chairs, clothes from several people's wardrobes, and my childhood bed frame. There are
paintings and photographs long since relegated to below eye and
ground level, a pinball machine in two pieces, magazines and books,
and games from before my birth. Trunks full of the stuff I left behind when I flew the nest remain unmoved, and there is furniture
enough for a small apartment. It all comes together in something
that resembles the storage area at the Smithsonian.

My father laments, out of earshot of my mother, the state of the
basement, but he knows that there is little he can do. He's battling
an ingrained need to keep things that's fueled by a heady mix of
nature, character, genetics, and probably some other things my
mother never threw out.

And that's what concerned me about Cleanliness. My mother's
capacity for accumulation may have been part of my DNA cocktail.
Franklin and I might have been battling the very forces of creation
in an effort to make me more virtuous. Perhaps I was simply not
predisposed to having an orderly habitation. Maybe I was doomed
to a life of "stuff."

I would soon find out.

Next to Godliness

After much reflection and rumination, I decided that the secret to
Cleanliness was . . . to clean. Each night I would select an area of
my house to tackle. Options abounded. My wife complains often

about the computer desk and the piles of paper, CDs, and various other items that have accumulated in that small three-by-six-foot area. The junk in my garage means that my car only fits in occasionally, and my clothes closet has become a museum-like collection of life's trinkets. The only real dilemma was where to start.

In one sense, the choice was obvious. Given how I began this chapter, could I commence my cleaning anywhere other than my closet?

I never gave a single thought to the amount of space I needed for my stuff until I was muscled out of the closet in the bedroom. Ostensibly I was to have half of our closet; however, the encroachment into my closet turf by my wife makes the Middle East conflict look positively sedate. Gradual advances—some clothes here, a book there—have led to massive and widespread incursions. There are girly things among my manly things, and this is cramping my style. For a while I had almost been prevented from accessing my work clothes by a giant green exercise ball.

Until Ben and his virtue of Cleanliness, I had accepted that I had lost the closet war. But now, armed with the excuse of the pursuit of moral perfection, I renewed hostilities in this conflict. I would take back what was once mine. I would repatriate my closet—or at least sort out my side.

As I began my sorting and rummaging through years of accumulated T-shirts, gym shorts, ties, and cuff links, I saw immediate benefits of the virtue. Not only was my closet looking decidedly less like a warehouse, but I had also found things—useful things. An unopened stick of deodorant (as opposed to an opened, used stick, which would have been a little gross), a miniature golf bag full of tees and ball markers, shoelaces, photographs of my children, notes made to myself about writing ideas, and a box full of never-attempted magic tricks.

Of course, all of these treasures were buried under a considerable amount of nonessential stuff. In the process of cleaning my closet, I filled two garbage bags and one fair-size cardboard box full of clothes for donation to a local charity (I can mark that down as a Good for the day), threw away nearly a full garbage bag of useless items, and discovered that I had more than enough room for what was left over.

As I was cleaning, an odd feeling came over me. I had a small sense of euphoria as I discovered that throwing things away sometimes brings things back. I'm back in the closet!

Okay, that sounded wrong.

I was just excited about seeing the floor.

Indeed, by the end of Day 1, I was feeling full of Franklinian virtue! Not since Order or perhaps Sincerity had I felt such a flush of enthusiasm for this project. The virtue of Cleanliness was confirming to me an important personal characteristic. Though I am emotional, sentimental, and a romantic (my wife would clearly disagree with this last trait), I am also a pragmatist. I appreciate the benefits of practical solutions over abstract concepts.

And as any business guru, successful sports coach, or motivational speaker will tell you, success breeds ambition. My Day 1 efforts to clean my closet had filled me with mad notions of the possible. Like Rocky after Mickey cuts him ("Cut me, Mick!"), I could see again. I could go the distance. I could be virtuous.

Indeed, I was so inspired that I decided to step up my cleaning efforts—take them to a new virtuous level. Instead of just cleaning willy-nilly, I would implement a real plan. I would be organized in my cleaning. First step, a surface scrub—get rid of the really useless (and in some cases slightly disgusting) stuff. Next, go a little deeper. Examine the items that were left, ditch any ideas of sentimental attachment, and divide them into piles: (1) things I definitely want to keep; (2) things I believe I can give away in a useful manner; (3) things about which I am unsure; and (4) things I have trouble identifying (or which are moving).

Once I had piles of materials in various states of wantedness (is that a word?), I would apply a level of analysis to my postpile organization. For *{ Trusting too much to* example, the wanted pile would get sub- *others' care is the ruin* divided into things that I could put *of many.}* away immediately (in a clean manner) and things that might need some further organizing or even culling.

Finally, once I'd organized and kept or discarded items, I could implement some ongoing scheme to ensure that I had a continuous cleaning program. That should make future projects more like tidying up, as opposed to postapocalyptic reconstruction.

Unfortunately, my construction of the plan took too long. I never got around to actually doing this "organized" cleaning. Despite this setback, I remained buoyant.

I might go to sleep in one of the closets to celebrate.

A Little Air out of the Balloon

Oh, this was all too good to be true. I was actually seeing real, concrete results. Cleanliness abounds. I almost didn't know what to do with myself.

Fresh from my closet-cleaning successes and new cleaning plan in hand, I decided to turn my Cleanliness efforts on my office at work, the computer desk in the basement, and my garage.

As with the closet, I discovered gems long thought lost, memories buried under piles of knickknacks, and projects forgotten and stored away. In the past I might have gotten caught up in a sentimental attachment to many of these treasures. In this case, however,

I was determined to apply one of Franklin's other virtues: Resolution. I was resolved that I would not hang on to things simply because they triggered a memory. Not every picture my children had drawn for me was a masterpiece, not every note poetry, not every photograph a keepsake. I would cull the herd in a Darwinian program of organization.

And again, it worked. I discovered that there was more than enough room in my garage for the car, I had plenty of old CD-ROMs that contained nothing of use, and my office had more than one reference book that was ten years out of date. There was simply no way to justify using reference materials that still viewed Y2K as an impending event of unknown consequences.

By the middle of the week, I was leading a much cleaner (or at least less cluttered) life. In fact, I was so enamored of my success that I decided to revisit my system of organization to see if I could impose some convergence of virtues—a little ethical cross-pollination. Mix a little Order with Cleanliness, add a dash of Resolution, and see what the brew tastes like.

Magnificent! Forty minutes of organizing emails paid off with an empty in-box, out-box, and deleted items. Never before in my career in government had I been so free of the tangled morass of unanswered, useless, will-sucking emails. My in-box was blissfully empty. I felt liberated.

My desk was similarly clear. I had jettisoned the detritus of ten years of accumulated files, stalled projects, and unwanted mail.

At the risk of sounding like I am bragging (Humility is coming up soon), I was all over Cleanliness. I was feeling virtuous. I had applied Franklin's virtue, and like a contestant on *American Idol*, I "made it my own." My closet, my garage, my computer, and my desk were all cleaner. I was happy. I should have been happy with being happy.

Instead, I was so pleased with myself that, against my better judgment, I let Michelle in on the nature of the weekly virtue.

"Did you notice that I've been cleaning?"

"Franklin again?" Her voice betrayed her disregard for my efforts.

"Yes. This week is Cleanliness, so I thought I'd tidy up. You know, clear out the clutter."

Michelle still seemed unimpressed. "Have you noticed a difference?" I asked.

Michelle looked up, and I knew when she smiled that she had set me up. "Not really," she answered.

Not really! I had cleaned half the house, donated items to charity, found things I had forgotten that I owned, and made more room for what was left. Not really?

"Ahhh," I told myself. "She's just jealous."

At least she hadn't suggested I move back into a closet.

And the Air Just Keeps Leaking

By Thursday I was downright pleased with myself. I had found a virtue that was showing immediate results (despite what Michelle might say). Here was a nearly three-hundred-year-old edict that still applied. Here was a precept with meat on its bones. In all my self-congratulations, I forgot Ben Franklin's Quaker friend, who, upon reading Ben's list of twelve virtues, proposed a thirteenth: Humility.

In the midst of all my cleaning, I made a quick visit to my doctor's office to have a prescription renewed. It wasn't meant to be a checkup—I wasn't even expecting to see my doctor. As I sat and leafed through a magazine, the nurse came in to take a quick history. This particular nurse is a lovely woman, but working in a busy medical practice, she is focused and all business.

She scribbled on my chart as she asked about my diet, my level of exercise, and my sleep patterns. As she took my recent medical history with a disinterested professionalism, I made several attempts at witty repartee. She seemed immune to my charms. Maybe she was laughing on the inside.

As she went about her tasks, I resisted the urge to tell her of my virtuous exercise. No sense in bragging, the efforts must have been obvious. Finally, she asked me to step on the scale. Confident and full of the knowledge that for more than two months I had been temperate, resolute, and moderate, I inquired whether I should keep my shoes on or take them off. I should have guessed what was coming when she, eyeing me up and down, said, "I would take them off if I were you."

Now you'll remember that I started this program at about 250 pounds. Over the passage of the previous couple of months I had attempted to find in Franklin's precepts the motivation to exercise more regularly, make better dietary choices, and generally adopt a healthier lifestyle. Despite occasional setbacks, I was convinced that, like Cleanliness, I was being at least moderately successful. I hadn't weighed myself—I was planning on saving that for the end— but I was sure that a little midcourse assessment could only provide the type of positive feedback that seemed to be in abundance this week.

As the nurse, that model of professionalism and Germanic sobriety, adjusted the sliding weights, I anticipated the good news.

"So," I asked as I stepped off, "what's the damage?"

Without looking up from her note making, she replied, "Two hundred and forty-five pounds."

I was stunned. This couldn't be right, I *assured* myself. Had not people been telling me how slim I looked? Were people not asking me how I had lost weight? Did I not feel better?

"I've been lifting a lot of weights," I said to the nurse. "Muscle weighs more than fat, doesn't it?"

She gave me a waiting-room-weary look and mumbled something like, "So they say," as she strapped on a blood pressure cuff. I was leery now. The weight thing had thrown me.

"They always use the larger cuff on me," I said. "I have big arms."

Another weary look, a number of pumps on the squeeze ball, and raised eyebrows. "Your blood pressure is too high," she said. No wonder, I thought, you've just told me all my efforts have lost me a measly five pounds. Her disappointment in me was obvious. It was as if I had failed her. She didn't even know that I was seeking moral perfection, and yet she clearly found me wanting.

And why wouldn't she? The truth was out. Even with all my self-deprecating jabs about my failures, I'm sure we all hoped at the conclusion of this story there would be a happy ending. But despite all our good wishes, there it was, visceral evidence of my failure to follow Franklin's virtues. This was more than a check on a chart or a vague sense of unworthiness—this was real, hard, irrefutable evidence that I was not following some or all of Franklin's virtues.

As I skulked out, prescription in hand, my heart was heavy with the knowledge that not only was I a failure but I would have to acknowledge my shortcomings to the world. So here is my acknowledgment.

{ *The absent are never without fault, nor the present without excuse.*}

I am no Benjamin Franklin.

He was at least forty pounds lighter.

A Little Cleanliness for the Soul

One would have thought that the opportunity to meet and speak with a man recognized as one of the world's leading humanitarians might be beneficial to a person seeking to be more virtuous. I can only blame your lack of understanding on some confusion over my character.

This section of the book requires an understanding of my contemporary ethical guide. As I have said, Chris Levan has a mind that works at somewhere near the speed of light. He juggles multiple projects, constantly thinks of new ventures in a myriad of arenas, organizes countless events, and lends his labor, both physical and mental, to almost any project he thinks would benefit from his help. Sometimes it can be a bit exhausting to watch for people like me, who are a little more temperamentally inclined toward watching rather than doing.

It was in this context that he approached me and another colleague and asked if we would chair a conference entitled "The Politics of Compassion." "Don't worry," said Chris, "I'll do all the work." From anyone else, I would've taken the statement as disingenuous. From Chris, I took it as gospel.

And he was good to his word. Chris, and a core team of volunteers drawn from the church where Chris is on the ministry team (and where I attend irregularly), handled almost every aspect of the two-day conference. Other than chair a few meetings—my chief responsibility, as I explained to the first-day audience—was to welcome people, introduce a few speakers, and point out the location of the washrooms.

Indeed, I felt a bit like a fraud. Several times over the course of the conference, participants would congratulate me on how smoothly things were running. I did my best to explain that I took no credit for anything, but try as I might, people could not be dissuaded from the notion that I was somehow responsible. Even some of the volunteers, the people who were doing the real work, suggested that

I should be proud of what had occurred. I maintained my humility and decried any attempts to foist glory on my shoulders.

And yet, by the time Mr. Stephen Lewis, the keynote speaker, was to give the first of his two addresses on Friday afternoon, I was feeling the tiniest hint of self-satisfaction.

That ended when Mr. Lewis actually spoke.

For those who don't know, Stephen Lewis is a former politician who has been the deputy executive director of UNICEF and the Canadian ambassador to the United Nations and, at the time of the conference, was UN Secretary-General Kofi Annan's special envoy for HIV/AIDS in Africa. He was appointed by the Organization of African Unity to a Panel of Eminent Personalities to investigate the genocide in Rwanda, and in 2005, *Time* magazine listed Lewis as one of the "100 most influential people in the world." He is, even to those who might not share his political views, an intellectual heavyweight and a humanitarian.

Lewis described, in his first talk, the politics of compassion in the context of his work trying to stem the tide of HIV and AIDS in Africa. It was a stark tale, full of death and misery, interspersed with anecdotes about his encounters with rape survivors, AIDS orphans, and genocidal militias. In the midst of all that, he described his own efforts and the efforts of others like him to put a halt to a disease with infection rates in some parts of the continent close to 50 percent. The common reaction to his talk was a sort of loose-jawed awe: the sense that, though you did not doubt his words, you simply could not believe the message. *How can so many be dying, in pain, tortured, and helpless and I have not lifted one finger to come to their aid?*

What was more humbling was that this man was doing something. He was dedicating his life to a mission, applying his passion, and not surrendering to the hopelessness that his experiences must have impressed upon him. And all I was doing was accepting false credit for bringing him to town (and successfully pointing out the location of the washrooms).

Things might not have been so bad had he not been scheduled to speak again that evening. The speech itself, once he delivered it, just reaffirmed my interest in his topic and my anxiety at my lack of a meaningful contribution. It was the prespeech meeting that really caused me problems.

Mr. Lewis was brought to Chris's office. Another member of the organizing committee and I had been given the task of entertaining him, more or less, while he awaited his turn to speak. The benefit, the quid pro quo, was that we had the opportunity to speak with him. I was mindful of the intrusions on Mr. Lewis's schedule and was determined not to bother him. Graciously, however, he invited some conversation. We talked of his university days, his father, and volunteering. I was invigorated, but at the same time I had a lingering sense of a lack of personal accomplishment.

I'm not sure it struck me at the time, but this is the very force that drove me to take up this virtuous journey—the notion that I just wasn't doing enough with my time on this mortal coil. Stephen Lewis was just inadvertently reinforcing that feeling.

I am not sure why I said what I said next. Maybe I sensed that this was a chance for some guidance—an opportunity to learn from a giant of virtue. Maybe I was just overwhelmed with the enormity of what he had been talking about at the conference. For whatever reason I said, "Mr. Lewis, as I get closer to forty, I am beginning to feel an impending sense that I should be doing more."

I'm not sure what I expected him to say. A little pep talk maybe, a gem of moral guidance. What he did say caught me completely off guard.

"How do you think *I* feel? I'm sixty-eight."

Here was this man of accomplishment—author, politician, activist, humanitarian, UN envoy, ambassador, philanthropist—expressing his own discomfort over his lack of achievement.

Everyone senses the ticking clock of mortality. Surely Franklin felt it as well. He was a great believer in the common good. He wrote: *"As we enjoy great advantages from the inventions of others, we should be glad of an opportunity to serve others by any invention of ours; and this we should do freely and generously."* That is the nature of Franklin's style of accomplishment, his idea of civic-mindedness—it is simply never enough.

You know by now that I am a believer in coincidence as evidence of the presence of something greater. Surely my few moments with Stephen Lewis, just as I was beginning to feel good about my efforts with Benjamin Franklin, were a reminder from . . . someone . . . that this course of virtues was about more than having a clean closet or a well-ordered desk. The pursuit of virtue was not a selfish journey for Benjamin Franklin, and neither, I was reminded, should it be for me.

CLEANLINESS

TOLERATE NO UNCLEANLINESS IN BODY, CLOTHES, OR HABITATION.							
	S	**M**	**T**	**W**	**TH**	**F**	**SAT**
Temperance				★		★	★★
Silence				★			★
Order							
Resolution							
Frugality	★	★	★	★	★		★
Industry			★	★			
Sincerity							
Justice						★	★
Moderation					★		
Cleanliness							
Tranquillity		★	★★★		★★★		
Chastity							
Humility							

CHAPTER 11

Tranquillity

Be not disturbed at trifles, or at accidents common or unavoidable

WHO REMEMBERS ANYTHING MORE CLEARLY THAN THE BIRTH OF THEIR first child? I was in my third year of law school, twenty-five, and barely mature enough to babysit a goldfish when Kelsey arrived. I was not fit to be a parent. But there I was, on the cusp of one of life's great adventures, unprepared, overwhelmed, and yet filled with expectation and hope.

{ *Content makes poor men rich; discontent makes rich men poor.* }

What I remember most are the plastic air hoses.

There had been some warning that Kelsey's birth might not be without drama. Months earlier, while I was working at a summer job about an hour from our apartment, Michelle passed a blood clot. At first we feared she might miscarry, but to our relief the pregnancy continued. Then, when she was just thirty-two weeks along, Michelle's water broke. The doctor was able to stop the de-

livery but put Michelle on her back in a hospital bed for the next
month. We were young and scared, and still didn't appreciate what
was coming.

When the obstetrician feared she could delay the pregnancy no
longer, she set a date for the birth: November 20, 1992. At 8:30
a.m., Michelle was induced.

By suppertime that night, we were still waiting.

It was apparent that things weren't going according to plan.
Michelle was in labor, but Kelsey wasn't making her appearance.
Worse, the fetal heart monitor was showing a heartbeat that was
causing clear distress to the delivery team. Finally, as Kelsey made
her way into the world, chaos (at least it seemed like chaos to me)
ensued. Instead of "It's a girl!" the only exclamations from the doctor were instructions to the neonatal intensive care nurses. Kelsey
wasn't breathing on her own, and I watched as a nurse, ironically
the wife of a law school classmate, assisted her breathing with oxygen from a wall-mounted life support system. Michelle was nearly
comatose from the medications she had received during the difficult
birth.

Ultimately, some command from the doctor caused the entire
delivery team to rush Kelsey from the room, warming bed and all.
They wheeled her away so fast that the tubes attached to the oxygen
mask pulled loose. They hadn't even bothered to disconnect them.
It was then that the seriousness—the desperation—of the situation
struck home. It is those tubes that are clearly and indelibly etched
in my memory.

And then I waited. For thirty minutes, I sat by Michelle's side
(she was blissfully asleep and less blissfully now battling some fever),
wondering if my newborn daughter was alive or dead. That was not
a good thirty minutes.

Finally, a nurse came and led me into the neonatal intensive care

unit and sat me in a chair in a corner. The room was full of new-
borns like Kelsey, too feeble or small or ill to begin life on their
own. All of them were hooked up to special monitoring equipment.
There was a constant cacophony of alarms. "Don't worry about
those," said the nurse, "they go off all the time. The doctor will call
you over when he is ready."

The doctor in question was bent over Kelsey's warming bed,
examining her intently. He poked and prodded her as I watched
from a distance, relieved that my daughter was alive but terrified
about what was to come next. Finally, he motioned for me to join
him.

The first words he uttered—the first thing he said to this frightened, confused, unprepared father—were not "She's going to be
fine," or "We're very hopeful," or even "This is your daughter." The
first words he said were, "Does anyone in your family have webbed
toes?"

Thus began our life with Kelsey.

Later that night, my parents took me out for a bite to eat.
Michelle was asleep, Kelsey was in the neonatal intensive care, and
I was exhausted and scared and confused. My parents tried to calm
my fears and ease my mind. As my mother, a very experienced
nurse, talked about some of what the future might hold, I said, "It
doesn't matter if she's physically handicapped (not even a word I'd
use anymore), as long as she isn't mentally handicapped."

All I can say to my past self is: "Watch out what you say."

The next few months were filled with long nights at the hospital
(one of us would always be there while Kelsey stayed in neonatal
intensive care), unanswered questions for the doctors (we were
awaiting the results of genetic testing), and hope—hope that our
very little girl (4 pounds at birth) with the fused toes, crooked fingers, and curly hair would be okay.

Kelsey came home the day before my first Christmas exam. She and I began a pattern of sleeping sitting up (me sitting up, Kelsey lying on my chest) because she couldn't keep her formula down while lying prone. It made for an interesting exam period and a different first Christmas than we had envisioned.

Finally, the month after Christmas, the pediatrician's office called to schedule an appointment. The genetic tests were back.

After giving our daughter a quick physical exam, the doctor suggested we sit down (never a good sign) and told us that Kelsey had a rare genetic problem. Her second chromosome was missing a section. The medical term is an interstitial deletion of chromosome 2q. The layman's explanation was that she had a problem so rare it had no name, was shared (at the time) by only seventeen people in the medical literature, and was likely a death sentence within the first year of life. In that year, he told us, her development would be profoundly delayed, and should she survive, she would likely never advance past one year intellectually.

I remember staring out the window of the doctor's exam room at the traffic flowing past on the busy street below and thinking, "Look at all those people with nice normal lives, and here I am with a special needs child who will die in a year. It's not fair."

I believe that was the one and only time I felt sorry for myself.

Kelsey did survive, though she kept us holding our breath on a few occasions. She developed epilepsy shortly after we moved for my first job after law school, and had her first seizure while friends visited from home. She spent nearly six months in a children's hospital an hour from the town in which we lived. Michelle lived at the hospital with her during the week, I would drive to visit them at night, then drive home late in the evening to be ready for work the next morning. On weekends we would trade roles. Ultimately, we decided we would have more support back in the city where we had both gone to college. Michelle and Kelsey made the move one week before I did.

On the day before my final bar admission exams, I got a call from Michelle in tears. Kelsey had reacted to one of her anticonvulsants, she was having trouble clotting, and the doctor was asking whether we wanted them to take heroic measures if she were to stop breathing. She wanted me to decide, as she was too upset. As I spoke to the doctor, he suggested I get there as quickly as I could.

For the entire four-hour drive, I expected to be too late. As I pulled into the hospital parking lot, I braced myself for what was to come. But then, through the windows of the entrance of the hospital, I could see my father sitting next to my close friend Stephen. They were talking, and more important, they were laughing. I knew that Kelsey was okay.

And she has been okay for more than sixteen years. There have been health crises, and as the doctors predicted, her intellectual development peaked at the level of a one-year-old. She can't walk or speak, and she is fed almost exclusively by a tube that goes directly into her stomach. But she is our daughter, she brings us joy, and she is okay.

Life, lemons, and lemonade—Tranquillity is a state of mind.

Every crisis with Kelsey has been like a link in a suit of chain mail for me. When things get tough, I think of what Michelle and I have been through. When I feel down, I remember how hard things have been and how much harder they could have been. Kelsey is my armor. Even when Michelle and I lost our second child less than an hour after her birth, I knew we would survive. Kelsey is my Tranquillity.

If I was ever confident about a week of Franklin's virtues, this would be it.

An Obsession with Tranquillity

We, as North Americans—the citizens of this globe for that matter—are a great seething ball of self-manufactured stress. For some, it is the stress to be successful; for others, the pressure of a relationship. For many, it is a simple but wrenching daily struggle to survive. That said, much of what stresses us comes from the nature of our commercial, market-driven, materialistic society. It's clear that we all need a little Tranquillity.

This is the virtue for which Franklin tells himself, and those who might follow: "Don't worry about the little things" (okay, that's not a direct quote, but you get the idea). As a man driven to achieve, Ben undoubtedly saw the need for some balance—a little peace to counter the push to succeed.

Even before Kelsey came along, I think I had a leg up on Tranquillity. My parents taught me that there are simply some things you cannot control, that most injuries (physical and psychological) are a long way from your heart, and that good things happen more often than bad. This is the one area in which I felt some sense of virtuous accomplishment. This is the one virtue in which I might educate rather than learn. I felt I should offer something practical— something more than vague platitudes. Being tranquil and teaching Tranquillity, however, are two very different things.

Can I articulate how I manage to be tranquil? What about Ben Franklin? Does he offer anything other than an admonition not to worry?

More than how to be tranquil, Franklin offers an example of why. His life was not without trials and hardships. He lived, of course, in a most unsettled time, but most of Franklin's tribulations and setbacks were a product of his own willingness to risk and lose. Leaving his hometown of Boston as a young man, he cast himself into the world with virtually nothing and yet eventually managed to become one of America's most influential citizens. He wrote in his autobiography of the contrast between the young man who arrived in Philadelphia, essentially penniless, and the man he was to become:

> I have been the more particular in this description of my jour-
> ney, and shall be so of my first entry into that city, that you may
> in your mind compare such unlikely beginnings with the figure
> I have since made there.

When he was settled in his new city, Franklin began the process of "making" himself. Eventually, on only the promise of credit from the governor of Pennsylvania, Sir William Keith, he crossed the ocean to London to buy supplies for a new printing business. When he arrived, he discovered that Keith's promise of credit was worth-less. Franklin was marooned in one of the world's largest cities with-out the means to support himself. Instead of panicking, he went to work for two printers, further educating himself in his trade and developing new and important relationships. This was the nature of Franklin when confronted with crisis or setback. He simply made the best of it and generally emerged the better for the earlier loss. These were the actions of someone who understood the Tranquillity he preached in his autobiography.

All that said, he isn't very specific about how one goes about not being disturbed at trifles. There are examples aplenty in his book about him forgiving slights or wrongs, but little about how he trained himself to do so. In Tranquillity, as in all the virtues, Franklin did not claim perfection, though he did suggest his descendants might well find that "to the joint influence of the whole mass of the virtues, even in the imperfect state he was able to acquire them, all that evenness of temper, and that cheerfulness in conversation."

Have his descendants (in the broadest sense) learned his virtue? Have they reaped the benefit of his self-help?

If you were a child, as I was, in the seventies, then when you think of finding Tranquillity, your mind leaps to peace symbols and flower power and Allen Ginsberg. Rather than notions of stoic acceptance of injuries and injustices, I picture protest marches and hippies and hear psychedelic rock. And ironically, that is where the seemingly insatiable American appetite for self-help, happiness, and fulfillment reached its zenith. Though its roots may lie as far back as Franklin and certainly as long ago as the middle of the 1800s, the apex of the American obsession with psychological health was in the "me" decade.

In her book *In Therapy We Trust: America's Obsession with Self-Fulfillment*,[1] Eva Moskowitz points out that in the 1970s, self-help books dominated the best-seller lists, and bookstores began to dedicate entire sections to works aimed at people seeking to get in touch with their feelings, express themselves, and find internal peace.[2] This generational obsession with the psyche would lead to games dedicated to feelings (the Feel Wheel),[3] untold numbers of self-help books (some with titles like *It's Me and I'm Here* or *I Ain't Much Baby—But I'm All I've Got*),[4] and therapy groups with dubious treatment theories. My favorite of these, as described by Moskowitz, was the Erhard Seminars Training, or est, which "emphasized experience, authenticity and emotional honesty" over "intellectualizing."[5] They did this, apparently, by charging $250 for sixty hours of training, during which they would call the trainees "assholes" and restrict their food, drink, and bathroom privileges.

Who could have believed this stuff would be helpful? How did primal scream therapy, therapeutic regurgitation, rebirthing, and nude encounter groups become mainstream enough to attract adherents by the thousands?

Of course, there's nothing wrong with New Age spirituality, but I can say without reservation that it is not for me. I don't like Yanni, I can't sit cross-legged, and I just don't have the patience to meditate (especially if it involves chanting a mantra over and over). I'm sure these things

{ *Write your injuries in dust, your benefits in marble.*}

work for some people, but they would have the opposite effect on me. After half an hour of chanting "ooohm" and seeking my center, I would be ready to shoot someone from a grassy knoll.

So Day 1 ended with me having achieved a dubious honor. Having spent the day considering Tranquillity, I can say, without reservation, I felt less tranquil.

Maybe I should have found a nude encounter group.

Anger Management for the Masses

Day 1 of Tranquillity hadn't proceeded as smoothly as I would have hoped. The problem, as I saw it, was that I'd been baited by Mr. Franklin on this one. He's dangled the tasty morsel of Tranquillity, but it's like eating canapés at a reception—good food, not very filling. I think we need to talk to some criminals.

My job is not the best place to seek Tranquillity. The criminal justice system may be a petri dish for the world, but the amoebas are angry. In fact, after addictions and mental health issues, anger is probably the most common cause of criminal activity. (I have no statistics to back that up, just a lot of experience.)

Part of the prosecutor's role in the justice system is to try and prevent offenders from reoffending. Almost inevitably in circumstances in which an offender commits an act (usually of violence) out of anger, I recommend, and they are sentenced, to a period of probation with anger management counseling (after whatever in-

carceration is appropriate). I've never really been sure what happens
at anger management sessions; I just rely on the probation officers
who tell me that it helps. Judging by the rates of recidivism, I've
never been totally convinced of its efficacy, but to paraphrase the
seventies self-help book, "It ain't much, baby, but it's all we got." If
anger management is good enough for the nefarious and the ne'er-
do-wells, I asked myself, why isn't it good enough for Ben Franklin's
virtues?

I contacted a victim services worker who administers our court-
ordered anger management course to both adults and youths. If
anyone could help with anger management, she could. She's a very
calming person—and accommodating. She agreed to meet with me
to discuss the program.

The first question was, to me, obvious: "How do you teach Tranquillity to someone who is at your course because he or she broke a
two-by-four across a friend's skull?"

"First," she said, "participants are told that anger isn't about anyone else. It is an emotion, and no one else is responsible. They need
to own the problem."

Hum. "Own the problem" has a certain 1990s business speak
sound to me, but I didn't want to be judgmental. "What happens
next?"

"Once participants are told that their anger is not the fault of
someone else, they are led through self-image exercises."

"What are self-image exercises?" I asked.

"They think back to their childhood, for example," she explained, "and consider which parent they are more like. Then they're
asked to think about who else has been a major influence. Then we
end that exercise with them trying to remember any major events
of their life, both bad and good."

Okay, I was warming up to this. I liked the idea of influences.

I've had some good ones, and I'm pretty anger free. Maybe I wouldn't be quite so tranquil if my influences had been less positive.

"Once participants have a firm understanding of where their anger comes from," she said, "we try to get them to recognize when it is making an appearance. Knowing how the body reacts when anger occurs is a key to controlling it."

That made sense, too. Maybe we were getting somewhere with anger management. I even felt better about my part in having people sent off to participate in the course. "Is that it?"

"No," she said. "One of the keys to anger management is learning to negotiate and communicate—particularly in conflict. Different negotiating styles are reviewed." Different negotiation styles? Oh, I don't like those words. An uncomfortable sense of déjà vu washed over me.

During my bar admission course, we were offered instruction in various negotiating styles. One of those, the one advocated by the bar course leaders, had as its central theme rejecting positional negotiating and trying to determine the real interests of the other party. After appropriate instruction we were paired off, given a fictional case to settle, and sent off to negotiate.

My opposite was a mature student. He had already lived life, done things, and been places. He understood the artificiality of the exercise and the inconsequential nature of the whole process. I, on the other hand, got wrapped up in the competitive aspect of it all. Contrary to our training, I staked out a position, made an offer substantially above that, and waited for the give-and-take I expected. Instead my opponent, when hit with my opening salvo, said simply, "Okay, deal. You want another coffee?"

I was taken aback. Not only was there no negotiation, but now I would have to go back and explain how I had ignored our course on interest-based negotiation and taken advantage of an old man.

Thus, when my anger management consultant talked about "different negotiating styles," it killed my interest in anger management as the key to Tranquillity. It's probably an excellent course, but like yogic flying, it's not for me.

I thanked my anger management consultant for her help, and as she was walking out, she said, "Maybe you'd like to sit in on a course sometime?"

I thought about it for all of five seconds before politely declining. Notwithstanding my feelings about the course generally, it seemed unwise. This is a small jurisdiction. Most of the people in the course would probably be there because I helped put them there. Such a course could not end well for me.

It might, however, make for an interesting test of their newfound anger management skills.

The Harrison Gunn Method of Tranquillity

My stab at anger management might not have been the magic bullet on Tranquillity that I was seeking, but it did get me thinking about the source of my own Tranquillity. The course leader had said that, as part of the self-image exercises, people were asked to consider the major influences in their life. If that works for people trying to find the source of their anger, why couldn't it help me deconstruct the place from whence my Tranquillity flows (that sounded like something you'd see on the Tranquillity websites I visited).

Of course, there are Kelsey and my parents, but there had to be more. When I think of my influences—the people who have helped me not be disturbed at trifles—I see a painting that hangs in my basement. It's not an expensive painting; in fact, I think it is a mass-produced lithograph. It is not a masterpiece—I don't even know who painted it. It is, however, one of only two things I was interested in having from my grandmother's effects when she passed away. To me it is priceless.

The painting depicts a small boy on a horse-drawn wagon crossing a stream near a grist mill. The boy is driving the team, and the old man beside him is leaning in and whispering words of encouragement. From the moment I saw the painting as a young boy, hanging on my grandparents' wall, it was my favorite in the world, and the boy was me and the man my grandfather. When I think of Tranquillity, I think of him.

Harrison Gunn was a giant in his day. At six-foot-six, he towered over others. Despite his size, however, he was the gentlest of men. He never spoke harshly of others, I never saw him lose his temper, and he never seemed to be unhappy.

Like other people who grew up in the twenties and thirties, he might have had lots of reasons to be unhappy. He was born, raised, lived, and died on the same country road on which his father, and his father before him, had lived and died. He was forced to leave school early—I don't think he made it past the sixth grade—to work cutting wood for local sawmills so that he could help support his family. He was never rich—the time and the place of his birth would not allow it. He never traveled very far. My grandmother (they had been together since grade school) never liked to travel. She grew up in the same small, rural settlement and seemed satisfied with her little slice of the world, so they stayed close to home.

So why was he happy? Why did he seem so at peace with himself? I've never thought much about it until now, and until Chris provided me with his take on the virtue of Tranquillity, I'm not sure I could have articulated it.

Chris told me that there are three principle stressors in the modern Western world: noise, technology, and the need for meaning. I buy that. Picture yourself in the middle of a busy city, trying to answer the hundredth email of the day, while consumed with feelings of existential self-doubt. Sort of sums up modern life. As I think back on my grandfather, it seems to me that he had the recipe for handling these stresses. Here is what I will call the Harrison Gunn formula for Tranquillity:

1. Find a hobby you enjoy and practice regularly. My grand-father loved to garden and to read. Dad once told me that if his father could have been anything, he would have been a farmer. He satisfied this unrequited dream with large household gardens, which provided much of the sustenance for his family. He grew vegetables and apples and berries and in his toil found pleasure. In books he found pleasure of another sort. For a man who worked in a paying job from the time before he was a teenager until his mid-seventies, books were his relaxation. I think they also provided that window to the world that he missed by being so firmly rooted to one place. Of course, it is not lost on me, when I think of the stressors of the modern world, that gardening and reading are activities of peace and simplicity. No noise, no technology, just peace.

2. Don't let your world be consumed by electronics. I'm not sure how conscious a choice it was, but my grandparents had almost no modern technology in their home. That was, of course, a product of their times, but even late in the twentieth century, they were Luddites of the best kind. No computers, no digital cable. In fact, my grand-parents watched almost no television. They watched the news and hockey. I don't remember anything else. As a

young boy, I was driven insane by their house—it was always so quiet. In hindsight, however, I might describe it as peaceful. There is something to be said for the absence of technology.

3. Finally, seek meaning in the present. My grandfather and I didn't have many deep, philosophical discussions, so my understanding of his belief system is based almost exclusively on what I watched him do. Though the product of a Scots Presbyterian family, he came to a sect of Christianity who called themselves Christians (the more pejorative local term was Go Preachers). They led an austere lifestyle, attended services in people's homes rather than at churches (thus the Go Preacher name), and had a fundamentalist understanding of the Bible. Apparently my grandparents found this too severe a manner in which to bring up children, so once their family arrived, they left the church. Ultimately, I'm not sure what my grandfather considered himself, spiritually speaking, or if he thought of it at all. I do know that he gave land to a small parish of the United Church of Canada, though I don't believe he ever attended a service (other than funerals) within its walls. He never spoke harshly of any other person, and he was the least judgmental person I have ever met. He raised his family to respect others, and he found meaning and purpose in his children and in nature.

So there was my recipe for Tranquillity. Perhaps it is too austere for most modern Westerners, but it was okay for my grandfather, so it's okay for me . . . at least in short bursts. I decided that this would be my formula for the rest of the week. I would follow my grandfather

{ *Anger is never without*
a reason, but seldom
with a good one. }

as much as I follow Ben Franklin: limited use of the computer, little television
(you'll remember my last attempt at
restricting TV in the house—I wasn't up
to another family mutiny), and as much peace and quiet as I could
handle.

I was just glad my grandfather didn't chant.

Don't Mess with Yanni

The rest of the week was as I had hoped—tranquil. The only problem with a peaceful week is that it's uneventful. Not necessarily
much to report.

I suppose that given my work, an absence of agitation, aggrava-
tion, and drama might be a real success. Come to think of it, it
might be a miracle. Indeed, just like my success with Cleanliness, I
was feeling a little smug about Tranquillity. After I had rather cava-
lierly sauntered through the week, I should have known that Ben
Franklin would not let me off so easily. I got a good old case of
comeuppance—Yanni style.

Every year the prosecutors in my jurisdiction gather as a group
at an annual meeting meant to be part continuing legal education
and part management update. If you asked the attendees, however,
they would almost all agree that it is, at its best, a social event. War
stories and cold beer, munchies and shared laments. With friendships renewed, there is a general feeling of relief, I think, to know
that others inhabit the same world as you, wake up to the same
problems, and go off to bed with the same mixture of hope and
horror that is the brew of the modern prosecutor.

This year, ironically, the agenda included a session on stress
management. As I described above, I have a healthy disregard for

the psychological sciences, a suspicion of New Age spirituality, and a high opinion of personal stoicism. "Cowboy up" is my family motto (well, one of them). The simple truth: My excuse for being so offhanded about Tranquillity beyond what I've already described is that I am not terribly empathic. I do not see the need for outside assistance to overcome life's little troubles. I need no purveyor of psychobabble to tell me to breathe deeply and own the emotion. I espouse a minimalist mantra for stress management. Cowboy up!

The afternoon of the stress management lecture arrived, and my jaded view of psychology overcame my fear of my superiors. Attendance at the event was not optional, and generally I would never disregard a mandatory work event, but this was stress management. Come on, I thought to myself, surely prosecutors don't need someone who has never looked a murderer in the eye during cross-examination to tell us how to cope. I was itching to be elsewhere.

The die was cast when my boss (you'll remember the Cobra . . . imagine now his views on the efficacy of a stress management afternoon) said, "Let's go golfing." Well, I reasoned, if your boss tells you to blow off a session, that's almost like a direct order. Besides, everyone knows that physical activity is stress relieving. All sorts of happy little endorphins flowing around like little Tranquillity bumper cars. Thus, my boss, me, and four other like-minded colleagues went golfing. What could be more stress relieving than the frustration of trying to knock a tiny round ball into an equally small hole across acres of real estate? As Robin Williams says, there's a reason they call a shot a stroke.

I'd be lying if I said we didn't have a good time. It might make for a better story if we got rained on, or someone wrapped a club around a tree. That, however, is not what happened. We might not have played very well, but we enjoyed a stress-relieving afternoon. As we returned to the conference facilities, it was with some confidence that we'd find a group of coworkers who would be required to admit the error of their ways and the brilliance of ours.

That's not what we found.

When we returned, to my surprise, my colleagues were effusive about the presentation. Great stuff, they said, best presentation of the meeting. To add some further context, I should point out that most of these people would, by experience or nature, have a similar view of the world as the Cobra and I. These are a group of people to whom an admission of anxiety is tantamount to an admission of weakness. We might bemoan the stressors in the system but never its effect on our own psyches. These are prosecutors, the lone wolves of the justice system, guardians of the public safety. Now they were talking like groupies at a Zamfir concert.

What had happened in the few hours that we had abandoned them? What body snatchers had invaded and replaced my battle-hardened friends with sensitive, New Age wimps?

So what was the big deal? I asked. One replied that they appreci-ated the Life Stress Chart, a stress value scorecard giving values to life's various events and circumstances. "I had no idea I had so many stressful things going on in my life," she added. Another liked a handout called "The Wear and Tear Syndrome of Stress."[6] The hand-out linked stressors to stress and then on to disease. "I've got to make some changes," my friend said. I thought I heard a note of desperation in his voice.

I thought about my week of Tranquillity. I had let Ben down. My own general sense of ease with the ebb and flow of life was easily replicated, I reasoned. People who complained about how stressful life is were just whiners. As I sat and listened to my peers, people who are anything but whiners, unburden themselves about how a two-hour course had shed a ray of light on their own battles with stress, I was overcome with a sense of guilt. How could I have been so callous?

It struck me, as I listened, that they weren't suggesting that there were great mountains of dismay weighing down on them. Rather, what they described sounded a little like being buried in sand on a beach. A few scoops of sand were just an irritant; a couple of buckets full, an uncomfortable weight but no more. Pile on enough sand, however, and the ability to move, freedom itself, was restricted.

Like sand at the beach, however, they also revealed that a little shift, some wiggling, and enough effort could loosen the sand. The more sand that was cast off, the less its hold on them. "I loved the strategies he gave us for coping with stress." This was the constant among the group. I decided I had better look at the materials they had been given.

As I examined the resources provided, I was struck with the simplicity of the solution for stress management that was offered. Tiny shifts, little movements, and the weight of the sand was lessened. And now, in the fullness of time, and following my examination of my own family members, the pattern was clear. Simplicity was the key. People generally lament the loss of the old times, but I don't think it is the past they seek. Rather, they want the simplicity of the past—the slower pace, the absence of constant stimuli, and the chance to just live. For me, these are the lessons of my grandfather and Benjamin Franklin.

I still, however, like golf.

TRANQUILLITY

	S	M	T	W	Th	F	Sat
BE NOT DISTURBED AT TRIFLES, OR AT ACCIDENTS COMMON OR UNAVOIDABLE.							
Temperance				★		★	★★
Silence				★			★
Order							
Resolution							
Frugality	★	★	★	★	★		★
Industry			★	★			
Sincerity							
Justice						★	★
Moderation					★		
Cleanliness							
Tranquillity		★	★★★		★★★		
Chastity							
Humility		★★	★				★

CHAPTER 12

Chastity

Rarely use venery but for health or offspring, never to dullness, weakness, or the injury of your own or another's peace or reputation

IF YOU'RE EXPECTING SALACIOUS DETAILS ABOUT MY SEX LIFE IN THIS chapter, you will be disappointed. After nearly two decades of marriage, I'm not sure I could even provide such details. Even if I could, however, I would not.

Indeed, the week of Chastity presented a unique problem and, perhaps, an opportunity. As a husband of many years—a devoted and loyal husband—Franklin's dictate to be chaste presented no serious difficulty for me. In fact, much like Moderation and Tranquillity, all I had to do was live my life exactly as I had been living it and Ben would be proud.

This, however, is not a book about doing nothing (notwithstanding my efforts at Tranquillity). This is a book about seeking virtue, about being better, about following in the footsteps of Ben Franklin. Franklin wrote about this virtue, and indeed all his virtues, in his old age. The course, however, if we accept Mr. Franklin at his word, was designed and used when he was a young man. And for a young man, Chastity might indeed have been a concern. Biographies are replete with suggestions, speculations, and innuendos about his dalliances. Certainly he was a man with an active sexual appetite. He acknowledges in some of his writings that he may have "consorted with low women." His son, William, was born out of wedlock, and the maternity of the boy has never been confirmed—indeed, it remains one of the few great mysteries of Franklin's life. In that respect, then, Franklin may have needed to work on the virtue of Chastity. I will not, for the sake of my mother, give any indication of whether or not this was ever an issue for me. I can say that since my marriage, it has not been.

What, then, does a loyal husband do—a husband seeking to better himself—when he is directed to work on the virtue of Chastity?

The answer might lie in my preparations for this course. In my precourse interviews I got, for the most part, answers that I had expected. There were no great surprises in people's perceptions of me. I was a bit taken aback by Michelle's description of me as a sloth, but in truth, I wouldn't have described myself as a cheetah (I still like stallion, but really, I'm just kidding myself).

The one answer I was truly not expecting, however, came from Michelle. She told me that I was a wonderful father but not such a great husband. How's that for honesty—brutal honesty.

Happily, she did qualify the answer. It was not that I was a bad husband but that I put my focus and my energies on the family unit as a whole. I was, and am, concerned with the well-being and happiness of my children. And, she acknowledged, I am good at it. What I am not so good at, she claimed, was our relationship. I was not dedicating the same sort of energy, interest, and focus to our relationship as a couple. She pleaded guilty to her own responsibility in that regard, but that didn't soften the blow. She was telling me, quite simply, that I was ignoring our marriage.

Now that could've been a showstopper right there. A smarter man might have said, "Forget this book, I have more important work to do." By now you are undoubtedly aware that I am not a "smarter" man. I forged on with this project, but at least I never forgot her response.

Where had I gone wrong? You'll remember my vision of myself as a romantic. I remember thinking as a teenager, after watching some television show or movie about a loveless marriage, that I would never find myself in such a situation. I made sure that dates, especially first dates, were memorable—a late-night picnic on an island in the middle of the river, a romantic dinner at an abandoned farmhouse, stream-side picnics at a secluded waterfall. After that, it was often a slow downhill slide.

Add to that complacency the everyday pressures and time constraints of raising children, gathering income, and simply living life, and the time devoted to the actual relationship gets short shrift.

The secret, according to experts, is hard work and focus, along with a commitment to the relationship. Trying new things together can also stimulate romance.

I SHOULD BE BETTER AT BEING A SPOUSE. I'VE HAD GOOD ROLE models. My parents communicate well, viewed (and view) their marriage as a partnership, and have managed to see and do new things together throughout their married lives. I'm sure they'll shudder when I hold them out as examples of what romance should be, but theirs is an exemplary marriage. My paternal grandparents were role models as well. They were together since they were essentially children.

But when I think of real-world romances, I think of my maternal grandparents. Hazen and Mary Dickson, like my paternal grandparents, met when they were little older than children. He was nineteen and she was seventeen when they married. Youth, however, wasn't their biggest problem. This was the 1930s, and Haze was a Protestant and Mary a Catholic. The community in which they lived, settled almost entirely by Irish Catholics and Scots Protestants, was not a place, at the time, of religious tolerance. Prejudices died hard, and theirs was not a marriage particularly welcomed by their families.

But they persevered, perhaps because of the struggles rather than in spite of them. They survived the death of a child and the Depression. They never made much money, but that didn't seem to matter. Their children and grandchildren viewed them as the center of the universe and a safe haven against all of life's storms. Theirs was a simple life, but it was a good one—one that they made together. On the tombstone that they share in the quiet country cemetery not far from their family home, the epitaph reads, "Life's Work Well Done."

That was the type of romance I had imagined as a young man. I had my example of what Ben Franklin meant by Chastity.

This, then, was to be the focus for the week's virtue. I decided to dedicate the week of Chastity to rekindling the romance in my own marriage. Not the fake, greeting-card-company romance, but the real-world, shared-mission romance. The type of romance that never gets made into a TV movie but that leaves a mark on the world, even if only a small one. The type of romance that would set an example for my own children.

The type of romance about which someone might say, "Life's work well done."

Operator, Can You Help Me Place This Call?

The secret to projects like this is to start small. Don't overextend yourself in the early going. To stretch the metaphor to a prize fight, you need to pace yourself in the early rounds, feel out your opponent, and settle in for the long haul. I decided to begin with a phone call.

One can never overestimate the impact of the unexpected phone call. The normal (at least in my world) daytime phone call between husband and wife concerns errands for the day, activities and children, or everyday complaints. A phone call for no purpose other than to describe how much your spouse means to you may be, I assured myself, an effective and simple way to begin the week of Chastity (as I had defined it). I made the call.

Strangely, it worked exactly as I had thought it might. My wife seemed genuinely happy to have had me call for no other reason than to say "I love you." I followed up the call with a conscious effort to remember in all circumstances how I had first felt about my wife. The effect, obvious to me because I was aware of my efforts, was instantaneous. We were partners rather than opponents.

Now, I don't want to give the impression that there is ongoing strife between my wife and me; there is not. There are, however, instances where our interests diverge. For the most part, these surround household responsibilities. There are children to be cared for and tasks to be completed. At the end of a long day, volunteers are hard to find. On Day 1, instead of shirking my responsibilities in such situations, I decided to be just such a volunteer.

Instead of delaying at the dinner table in hopes that Michelle would do the dishes, I sprung into action. Before she had a chance to lift a finger, the kitchen was clean. Then came the myriad of activities that surround putting young children to bed; any non-parents out there should imagine cattle herding on a tricycle. Our routine is complicated by Kelsey, who is now physically a teenager but remains an infant developmentally. Her activities of personal care require time, a strong back, and patience. But I was up to the task. Finally, there was the postbedtime downtime. Generally this consists of literally falling on the couch,

{ *A single man has not nearly the value he would have in a state of union. He is an incomplete animal. He resembles the odd half of a pair of scissors.* }

remote in hand, and eventually waking up with drool running down one's cheek and an infomercial blaring. On Day 1, however, I made some effort to see to my spouse's comfort before my own. A cup of herbal tea and an offer of whatever else she wanted. I was solicitous.

And I could tell it was appreciated. There were no outward displays of gratitude, but certainly there was a general sense of calm where normally there might be the stress and conflict of the children's bedtime ritual. Maybe Franklin was on to something here. I decided not to press my luck on the first day. Day 2 would be telling.

Red, Red Wine, Goes to My Head

Day 2 provided a strange twist in my week of Chastity. I had nothing special planned. In fact, planning would be almost an impossibility. There were conflicting schedules—Michelle going somewhere one night, I somewhere different the next, soccer for the girls, a soccer skills and drills session on the weekend, a promise to do yard work for my mother-in-law. It seems that in the modern family, there is very little time that is not scheduled. This, of course, is part of the problem with maintaining a positive relationship with a spouse. The second night of this virtue seemed to present just such a problem. My wife reminded me that we had agreed to talk about finances and home renovations—hardly a task that inspires romance. Bemused expressions and occasional angry words maybe, but usually no romance.

On this week of Chastity, however, a strange thing happened on the way to our conversation—we actually talked. After the kids were in bed, my wife produced a bottle of red wine and said, "I thought this might help things run smoothly." Indeed it did. Instead of the rancorous, vexing, anxious conversation that often accompanies the subject of money, we had a long, pleasant, calm conversation about everything from the actual topic at hand to how people achieve happiness and my wife's plans for the future.

This was the type of communication on which studies of successful marriages place such emphasis. This was real talking. It reminded me of how we talked when we first became a couple—like two explorers planning a grand adventure. And isn't that the spirit of hope and dreams that should pervade a marriage?

And I wasn't the only one who appreciated the tone of our talk. At some point Michelle made the comment that it was nice to just talk and that we didn't do it enough. Now, I am not suggesting that every conversation between husband and wife should be lubricated by red wine or should be about life's grand ambitions; there are dogs to walk and dry cleaning to be picked up. It's just that in between the dogs and the errands there has to be something more.

Despite my pleasure at the evening's conversation, I found myself slightly suspicious at my wife's motives. She knew nothing, I thought, of the particular virtue of the week, but this seemed almost too coincidental. Could she have seen through my Day 1 activities? Or was she reading my virtue diary?

Finally, I dismissed my suspicions. Coincidence or design, what did it matter? We had conversed amiably about the most contentious of marital topics and turned it into a pleasant talk about the future. That was enough for me. This Chastity thing was working out far better than I had hoped.

You've Got Mail

Chastity was moving up in the favorite virtue sweepstakes. Though it was a work in progress, I was already seeing the benefits. A greater concentration on my marriage was paying early dividends. I needed to keep up the pace.

A bit of inspiration hit me while I sat idly at my desk. I decided to send Michelle a message thanking her for the conversation from the night before. I composed a short note and sent it, via email, to our home computer. Here is what I wrote:

Hi

I enjoyed our talk last night. You're absolutely right that we need to sit down and talk more often.

We are raising a beautiful family and have a great life but we need to make sure that by the time our kids leave we are not strangers to each other. We should set aside time every week for each other.

Thanks for being a great wife and a great mother.

Love
Your Husband

Now, I should point out that a note like this could go either way. You've met my wife. She is a practical woman with plenty of experience with me. Instead of the legitimate and sincere note of love that I intended this to be, she might view it as the first salvo in a battle to obtain some marital pass, like a golf weekend—I am not above such chicanery. For several hours I received nothing in reply, and I feared the worst. Did she see mischief in my intentions? Was she angry that I had ruined the spirit of the previous evening? Was she suspicious that this had something to do with the book and was offended at seeing our personal life as fodder for my stumbling efforts at virtue (which, of course, it was—though I sincerely meant what I said and my purpose was noble)? Had she even checked the email? Finally, near the end of the workday, I received this reply:

Hey Cameron,

Surprised to get an email from you. I had fun too but the next time only one glass of wine for me or maybe a corona on a hot day. You're the best even though I give you a hard time.

Love ya, Michelle

Wow! That was exactly the response I had hoped for. I had made her happy. This Chastity thing was too easy. Given my experience with the virtues to this point, I should have known I was too smug. Fate can't let such an opportunity pass it by. I was in for yet another lesson.

The secret of Ben Franklin's system, as I thought from the beginning, is that it encourages the forming of new habits. The concentration on one virtue to the near exclusion of others builds a sort of virtuous muscle memory. You get so used to doing something that it becomes natural, almost instinctive. The problem with that formula is that you actually have to do the thing (or not do it, as the case may be) to form the habit. The foot must, most decidedly, remain on the gas. No coasting in this exercise. I should have learned that from Tranquillity. Yet as with the last virtue, once I started to feel good about myself, I took the virtue for granted. I started to coast.

As with the problems I had encountered in the late stages of the other virtues, I blame my early success. Like a hockey team that gets up a few goals on an opponent, I decided to play more conservatively. Wait out the clock and celebrate the victory. Maybe it was just the nature of my life. Remember, I am Mr. In-Between. I am not a risk taker.

On Wednesday, I had made a long-standing commitment to play a friendly game of poker with some friends after the kids went to bed. That was my first mistake. Michelle is not opposed to poker. Indeed, she likes me to have fun with my buddies. She hates it, however, when I lose (and when you play poker like I do, loss is an inevitability). Even the loss of twenty bucks (my maximum) sticks in her craw. That turns poker from harmless amusement to a gratuitous drain on family finances.

I'm sure quite a few of you are shaking your heads (and not for the first time), thinking, "What was he thinking?" I had committed to a week of being a better husband, and here I was going out to play poker? It gets worse. I lost.

I would do better tomorrow, I told myself. Again, I lied.

The next day, there was soccer for the girls. Now being a good father (usually), I had agreed to (assistant) coach Harper's team this year. This was my third year doing so. That, one would think, would not be a problem. Indeed, my wife supports the idea wholeheartedly. It does, however, cut into couple time. But so long as it is in the pursuit of our children's happiness, I would not notch this down as a transgression on the Chastity table.

However.

Taking the girls for an ice cream after soccer and coming home almost two hours postbedtime with two tired, cranky, sugar-filled youngsters did nothing to endear me to my wife. She offered the ultimate rebuke when we returned home: "You know better than that."

Scolded like a child, I wondered if I could redeem the week. Could I dust off the recriminations that had been justifiably heaped on me and surprise my wife again? Not likely. Perhaps it is my

{ Marriage is the most natural state of man, and . . . the state in which you will find solid happiness.}

nature to be a devoted father, but a not-so-devoted husband. Where was the romantic who frolicked beside waterfalls, who rowed canoes through the midnight waters of an ancient river, who read poetry by candlelight?

At the moment that I was asking myself these questions, *he* was watching the Stanley Cup Playoffs.

Where had I gone wrong? Of all the weeks, given what was at stake, why could I not rise above my infuriating ability to muck things up and truly be virtuous? My attempts to change that were coming to naught—I was blowing it. I was allowing the very things that had hampered me in the past be anchors on my voyage of virtue.

You Ain't Seen Nothing Yet

As I struggled through the last days of Chastity, I tried, in vain, to up my game. I took on household chores that I might normally avoid like an influenza outbreak, I did yard work for my mother-in-law (actually, I got to use a big saw doing the yard work, so that was really more for me), and I even assisted an accident victim (all right, that had nothing to do with Chastity, but I was grasping here). Despite these efforts, I could not replicate the early success of the week. The fates, soccer schedules, work, and a poor imagination all conspired against me. Finally, by Friday of the week of Chastity, I'd had enough.

Maybe the problem, I reasoned, was that I was in this thing alone. A relationship is, after all, a two-person dance. If only one person knows that the steps have changed, there are bound to be a few toes stepped on.

On Friday morning I called Michelle about some household renovations we had been discussing. During the course of the conversation I decided that it was time to let my dance partner in on the new tune.

"Did you know," I inquired gingerly, "that this week was Chastity in my Ben Franklin virtue course?" When she replied in the negative, I explained my plan for the week.

"I decided that I would take you seriously when you said that I was not always dedicated to being a good husband. So this week I decided to work on being a better husband."

"Really," she replied, "I hadn't noticed."

I gathered myself and, with as much dignity as I could muster, asked, "Didn't you notice the calls to tell you that I love you, the extra chores, the email telling you what a great wife you are?"

"I wondered what that was all about," she said. "I thought you wanted something."

I had! I had wanted to become a better husband. I had wanted to make this virtue about fixing one of the most concerning aspects of my precourse preparations. I wanted my wife to think of me in the same way that my children think of me. I wanted to be Superman to my wife.

Instead, I felt more like Clark Kent adjusting his clunky glasses. Virtuously speaking, I was clearly no superhero. The most my efforts had produced was suspicion from my wife. Not affection, not appreciation, not romance, just suspicion.

But did I really deserve anything other than suspicion? My focus on my relationship was unfocused and ill-planned. What early success I had achieved I squandered with self-centered and, sadly, all too typical behavior. No Superman indeed.

At least this would make the virtue of Humility easier to stomach.

CHASTITY

RARELY USE VENERY BUT FOR HEALTH OR OFFSPRING,
NEVER TO DULLNESS, WEAKNESS, OR THE INJURY OF YOUR
OWN OR ANOTHER'S PEACE OR REPUTATION.

	S	M	T	W	Th	F	Sat
Temperance	★★★★		★	★	★★★	★	★
Silence							
Order			★				
Resolution			★				
Frugality		★			★★		
Industry				★			
Sincerity	★★	★				★	
Justice						★	
Moderation	★★★★		★	★★			
Cleanliness		★			★		
Tranquillity					★		
Chastity	★			★★	★★		★
Humility			★	★	★	★	

CHAPTER 13

Humility

Imitate Jesus and Socrates

REMEMBER HIGH SCHOOL? THAT GREAT SEETHING GALAXY OF hormones, emotions, angst, and drama? I remember my first day, walking through the front doors and making my way to the cafeteria, where a thousand other students milled about like a great herd of wildebeests fearing the arrival of the lions. It was Day 1, and I was a skinny, pimply fifteen-year-old. And I was afraid. As I stood among the other wildebeests, my hope—my most fervent hope—was that no one would notice me. Or at least not beat me up. It was one of the worst days of my life.

{ He that falls in love with himself will have no rivals. }

It was one of the best days of my life.

That first day might have been a day of fear and anxiety and an overwhelming desire to run screaming from the school, but it gave way to the next day, which was better, and the next, which was better still. As time passed, there were sports and activities and girls and friends and dances and everything good that high school can bring. The bad came, too, of course—broken hearts and broken friendships and disasters great and small. These lows, however, were fewer and less memorable than the highs. Overall, high school was a fantastic experience.

That is, if you don't count the day my favorite teacher staged an intervention for me.

One day in the twelfth grade, this teacher, my teacher, took me aside and said, "Cameron, you like yourself too much."

That was Bob Gillis. He understood kids, he listened to us, and—perhaps most important—he cared. He wasn't being mean or vindictive when he told me I was arrogant. He was trying to help. So when Bob (which is what he let us call him) warned me of my conceit, I should have paid attention. Every neuron should have been thinking of ways to right this character flaw. It should have been a watershed moment.

I'm not even sure it dented my ego armor.

I did not become more humble that day. I did not become more humble that year. I don't know that I ever became more humble. The plain, simple, sad truth is that I have never mastered the virtue of Humility. I understand its need, its benefits, and the dangers associated with its opposite vice. But just as I cannot stop eating chips, I cannot (or will not) avoid liking myself. I probably could have written one of those seventies-era self-help manuals: *I Like Myself and I Don't Care What My Teacher Thinks.* Maybe I could combine it with a nude encounter group.

So, then, Humility was a virtue that offered both hope and fear. It was certainly an area that offered the greatest possibility for improvement. Yet if my favorite teacher couldn't stop my ego train, what chance did Ben Franklin stand?

One would think that after the previous twelve-plus weeks I'd have had this virtue locked down. The problem with arrogance, however, is that it does not dwell in the land of logic. It makes us believe the unbelievable. Despite ample evidence of failure, I had a steadfast, resolute, unswerving, and wholly unreasonable belief in myself. That is good. Confidence and self-esteem are the keys to success. But the universe is a place of balance. Too much of one quality and too little of another and the universe is without equilibrium. The yin to the yang of confidence is Humility. I needed a little of that yin to restore my balance.

Fortunately, Ben offered some specific guidance on this virtue. He said in his autobiography:

> My list of virtues contain'd at first but twelve; but a Quaker friend having kindly informed me that I was generally thought proud; that my pride show'd itself frequently in conversation; that I was not content with being in the right when discussing any point, but was overbearing, and rather insolent, of which he convinc'd me by mentioning several instances; I determined endeavouring to cure myself, if I could, of this vice or folly among the rest, and I added Humility to my list.

There is a hint of Bob Gillis in that Quaker and a hint of me in Franklin. On this issue, as with difficulties surrounding Order, Ben and I share common traits: pride, being overbearing, insolence. We are like hubristic doppelgangers.

Like me, Franklin also acknowledged his difficulty in mastering Humility:

> In reality, there is, perhaps, no one of our natural passions so hard to subdue as pride. Disguise it, struggle with it, beat it

down, stifle it, mortify it as much as one pleases, it is still alive, and will every now and then peep out and show itself; you will see it, perhaps, often in this history; for, even if I could conceive that I had compleatly overcome it, I should probably be proud of my humility.

{ *Pride that dines on vanity, sups on contempt.* }

It's a virtuous catch-22: Be humble, feel good about being humble, realize you're not being humble, start all over.

Franklin did offer some explanation of how he achieved a modicum of success achieving Humility. He faked it. He claimed no success in achieving Humility, but he did achieve a significant measure of success in the *appearance* of Humility.

That hardly seems virtuous, but it does have the distinct advantage of being more successful than whatever I'd been trying for the last forty years or so. So I would follow Franklin. I would adopt a respectful, diffident, restrained manner of discourse. I would make an effort to deny myself the pleasure of correcting the errors of others and thus at least achieve the appearance of Humility.

I hear a tinge of boastfulness in that pledge—I'd watch that.

The Four Stages of Learning and a Little Humble Pie

Perhaps, I reasoned, the way to begin a quest for Humility was in the precept to Franklin's virtue: Imitate Jesus and Socrates. It is one of the most direct pieces of guidance in the entire course.

I talked to Chris about this. Remember that among Chris's many hats, one of the most prominent is being a minister. In fact, he has a PhD in theology. Of all the virtues, here was the one for which I was certain he could point me down a safe and well-traveled road. I even had some notion he would be excited that I might seek guidance on how to follow Jesus.

Instead, Chris provided me a cautionary tale about Humility.

"Two years ago," he told me, "I went to pick up a babysitter, and when she opened the car door, I noticed she was sporting a new, bright yellow plastic bracelet, and it had the letters 'WWJD' printed into the band. I had no idea what the inscription meant, so I asked."

These bracelets are everywhere. You know the kind. They range from advertisements for bands or sports heroes to secret codes for dating emergencies to charitable promotions to awareness campaigns for debilitating diseases.

Chris continued, "When I asked what it was, the babysitter smiled, knowing I was a minister, and replied proudly, 'WWJD . . . It means: "What Would Jesus Do?"' She went on to explain that the bracelets were part of her youth group Bible project. They had decided as a group that they would wear these wristbands to remind them of an important principle. Whenever they were uncertain about their action, or whenever they were facing a decision that was novel or difficult, they would ask themselves, 'What would Jesus do?'"

Sounded exactly like what I should be asking, at least on this week. One had only to follow the direction Jesus led. That's exactly what Franklin advised (as had many others before and after him). Franklin's final virtue directs us to imitate Jesus. To be ethical, we have only to ask ourselves what he would do and then do the same. Virtue is a matter of imitation.

"But it's not that simple," said Chris.

Great, I thought. It all sounded very simple a few moments before. So why was it not so simple? What Chris said was that imitation is a poor basis for virtue. "Imagine," he said, "if I was to suggest that you imitate Mozart. You can't do it. Mozart was pure gift."

Imitation leads, Chris cautioned, to dependence and immaturity. If we are constantly gauging our behavior by our perception of another person's actions, we fail to grow our own intellectual and spiritual strength, we fear having a novel thought, and we allow our own ethical maturity to lie dormant.

For once, I might have been ahead of the curve. Promising, as I did, not to make this a book about religion, I do not need to digress too deeply into my own spiritual past. Suffice it to say that I was raised and remain a Christian, but I've never been too doctrinaire about it. I decided I wouldn't be slavishly imitating anyone. I still, however, needed to do something.

Chris offered a little more advice and explained that there are four stages of learning, and Humility is a key component.

First: "I don't know that I don't know." We all start off not aware of what is beyond our comprehension. This seems all too familiar.

Step 1 quickly leads to Step 2. When Step 1 is revealed to us, if we accept the truth of it, we are struck by our inadequacy and we whisper, "I now know that I don't know."

This, Chris told me, is where Humility is key. If we revert to a position based on the fear of looking stupid and defend our original misinformed belief, then we will never get further.

"I don't know that I know" is Step 3, a place Chris describes as the wilderness of unknowing, a frightening transition time during which we wander without direction, searching and hoping for a pathway—a place where we are closer to our goal than we realize. It is an intuitive place, where we must trust in our intuitive self to guard us from misplaced boasts and misguided presumptions. If we do, we may move on to Step 4, the final stage—when the light comes on and we finally can say to ourselves, "Now I know that I know."

So there I was, somewhere in the first stage of learning, expecting very soon to "know I don't know" anything about Humility, when once again, I was offered a real-world lesson on virtue. This time it came from the imagination of a twelve-year-old boy.

Several years ago my cousin, a woman who lives thousands of miles away and whom I see only every decade or so, was injured in a car accident. It was a serious accident, and she and her husband were lucky to survive. Sadly, she was left permanently disabled. Kathy, at just over forty years old and the mother of a young boy, was blind.

It is with some shame that I acknowledge that I did not one thing for her. Not a get-well-soon card, not a call to say I was thinking of her. Nothing. Wrapped up in my own busy life, sheltered by the miles between us, I did no more than offer sympathetic platitudes when my mother gave me periodic updates on her condition. It was not one of my bright, shining moments.

Then, two years plus after the accident, and in the midst of my final week of Franklin's virtues—a week devoted to Humility—I received the following poem written by her twelve-year-old son.

BLIND

The blind, you think they are slow
You think they are stupid
But they are just like you, they are very intelligent, they have lives
They are hard to understand because they have to learn—they are
very odd, but if you get to know them, they will tell you a story
So don't look at them strange and don't call them stupid
they are already learning how to read—learning how to read
  bumps is kind
of hard—you think they are just people trying to make a living in

the world,
so try and cut them slack.
There is no such thing as stupid or rolling your eyes
because they can't see you so the joke's on you
If you roll your eyes they won't care because
they can't see.
They don't care if you make fun of them and they
don't care if you call them stupid, so if you think they are stupid
you're going to get the same reply—wait your turn please.

Here was a boy who had moved way past "I now know that I don't know." I'd say he is in that brief shining moment when he can say, "Now I know that I know."

How's that for making you humble? How's that for a lesson in Humility?

Great Teachers, Bad Students

As anyone who made it through college or even just high school knows, there is simply no way to overstate the importance of a good teacher. A good one can make a dull subject palatable and a subject of interest a thing of wonder. A bad one can turn a student off a particular subject or learning in general.

I remember my first college English course. I had been a successful student of English in high school, but after my first Introductory English exam, on which I received a grade of B–, I was concerned that my success had been illusory. Determined to understand how I dropped from the lofty marks of high school English to a rather pedestrian B–, I visited the professor in his office. He looked a little like Doctor Octopus from *Spider Man*, if Doctor Octopus were dressed in a wool sports coat with accompanying turtleneck and spoke like Anthony Hopkins in *Remains of the Day* (that movie wouldn't come out for a decade or so, but that's how I remember him).

I explained that I was not disputing my mark, just seeking some explanation. "It's not that I'm saying I didn't deserve the B–," I explained, "it's just a bit of a surprise. I was an A student in English in high school."

He looked at the paper, peered up at me as if he had never seen a creature like me before, and asked, "And what high school did you attend?"

"Miramichi Valley," I replied.

Letting his eyes drift back to his work and handing me back my exam dismissively, he said, "Well, that explains it, doesn't it?"

I never enjoyed another English class.

On the other hand, I also had some good teachers—some very good ones. Mark Milner, a professor of military history, made his lectures come to life. When he spoke about sailors manning the watch on a Corvette plying the North Atlantic during World War II, I could almost feel the cold saltwater stinging my face. Talks on Renaissance art from Gary Waite made me want to visit Italy—or paint a naked woman (well, Gary's lessons were a nice justification).

What does all this have to do with Ben Franklin? Well, Franklin's precept for Humility, as we know, suggests imitating Jesus and Socrates. I'd already had my brief run-in with the Big Fellow, so I thought, despite Chris's warning against imitation, that it was time to give ol' Socrates a try.

The problem was that I didn't know the first thing about Socrates. I had a vague memory of him from a single classics course. I also ran into him in philosophy until I dropped the course. Another encounter with a bad teacher and so endeth Cameron the philosopher.

Classics was better. And again, thank the teacher.

Dr. James Murray, my classics professor, was still at my alma mater. He was, by the time of the week of Humility, the Dean of Arts, and since that classics course twenty years ago, our paths had not crossed. Still, if he straightened me out on Socrates once, then surely he could do it again. Despite being in charge of a faculty of thousands of students, he took my call. The best teachers are the ones who want to teach.

"When did you say I taught you?" Dr. Murray asked when I'd explained my dilemma.

"About twenty years ago. It was a first-year classics course."

"I've had a lot of students since then," he said. "Anyway, how is it that I can help?"

After giving him an idea of Benjamin Franklin's course of virtues and his precept for Humility in particular, I asked, "Why would Franklin want us to imitate Socrates?"

"You know," he said, "almost everything we know about Socrates comes not from him but from his students. Plato in particular in his *Dialogues* gives us the fullest account of Socrates. What we do know is that Socrates considered himself a teacher, but not in the sense that he was imparting knowledge. He viewed his role as something like a midwife."

Dr. Murray directed me to *The Theaetetus*, one of Plato's *Dialogues*, in which Socrates speaks of his role as a teacher. That was where he, through Plato, described his function as akin to being a midwife. Like a midwife, he could see when a student was having trouble giving birth to an idea. His purpose was not to give knowledge; it was simply to help with the delivery.

On Humility, it seemed that Socrates was of the admission-of-ignorance school; I suppose he probably invented it. That, at least, was consistent with Chris's four stages of learning. But that wasn't

really what interested me about what Dr. Murray said. The theme
that I kept coming back to was this: Socrates was, above all else, a
teacher. (I should note that he was an unpaid teacher and was ultimately tried and sentenced to death for teaching. Where were the
teachers' unions in ancient Greece?)

That was the missing piece, the
common element, the theme that
bound up Jesus, Socrates, and Benjamin Franklin. They were all, in their
way, teachers. That was what Humility
was for me.

{ *He was so learned that
he could name a horse
in nine languages; so
ignorant that he bought
a cow to ride on.*}

For Franklin, I decided, Humility—imitating Jesus and
Socrates—was about being a teacher. Had I done that? Had I been
a teacher? No, I didn't think so. Instead, I had been taught. I thought
back over the week. Chris had taught me about Jesus and the four
stages of learning. My cousin's twelve-year-old son had taught me
about tolerance and Humility, and finally, Dr. Murray had tied
the entire week up in a nice big bow.

Of all, I think I appreciated Dr. Murray's lesson the most. Not
because of what it told me about Socrates but for what it compelled
me to do next. Dr. Murray's lesson was responsible for my last act
as a devotee of Benjamin Franklin.

My last Franklinian gesture was a telephone call to a teacher to
say thanks.

An Apple for the Teacher

I love the symmetry of life—the way things come full circle. There
is something satisfying and poetic about a resolution that takes the
long view to appreciate. Thus, I decided that my course of Franklin's
virtues and, particularly, my week of Humility needed a spectacular

finish—a symmetrical, symbolic ending to a virtue that has been my undoing for nearly four decades. Given that the last week was the week of Humility, the course should end with gratitude.

I reached into my past, into the days when I had strived too hard to be somebody, to offer a long overdue thank-you to the teacher who made an effort to take a long view of my potential. I had started the week of Humility with Bob Gillis on my mind—Bob, who had gone beyond the simple obligations of curriculum and course materials and tried to teach me a real life lesson. I'm sure my vice of arrogance was apparent to all of my teachers, but he was the only one who pulled me aside and tried to teach me the virtue of Humility—to teach me that achieving Humility raises us above our base selves. He tried to get me to recognize the benefit of communal living, of shared experience, of our place in the grand scheme.

In this week of Humility, I decided it was time to let Bob know what that gesture, and he himself, had meant to me.

"Hello, Cameron, it's good to hear from you." It was a pleasant start, and as we shared bits of our recent history, I was reminded of why Bob was my favorite teacher. He understood us, our needs and desires, our frustrations at being restrained from running headlong into the wide world that lay before us. He loosened the reins just a bit (and in my case, snapped them back at least once).

"Bob, the real reason I'm calling is to say thanks." I had never done this before. I had never called someone to offer thanks for something done years before. It felt awkward but, at the same time, strangely right. "I wanted to thank you," I repeated.

"For what?" he asked.

Here it was. The circle was closing. A lesson had finally been learned and was about to be acknowledged. "Do you remember," I asked, "taking me aside and telling me that I needed to be more humble?"

There was only the briefest of pauses before he replied, "No, not really."

"Oh." I was stunned. "I see." I couldn't think of what else to say.

Why had I thought that this instant in a school hallway was as important a moment in his life as it had been in mine? I could remember where we were standing, what his exact words were, how I had felt at that instant. For him, I realized, it was just one moment in a career of teaching. Why did I think he would remember? I considered his answer for a moment and then understanding began to dawn.

"Bob, did you give these little gems of advice to a lot of students?"

"Oh, sure," he replied. "Sometimes I would see someone who needed a little kick in the pants and so I'd tell them what was what. Adults don't tell kids what they need to hear enough."

And I realized that the moment truly had come full circle. The lesson was really now complete. Only my own self-centeredness—my hubris—had led me to believe that this was a watershed moment for anyone other than me. I was so arrogant that I thought this was some priceless counsel passed to a favorite student. In truth, it was just one bit of friendly advice among many from a caring teacher. A kick in the pants for someone who needed it. I wasn't the hero of this episode; Bob was.

Now *that* was a lesson in Humility.

Thanks, Bob Gillis. Thanks to all my teachers. Thanks, Benjamin Franklin.

HUMILITY

IMITATE JESUS AND SOCRATES.							
	S	M	T	W	Th	F	Sat
Temperance		★				★	
Silence				★			★
Order			★				
Resolution		★★			★★		
Frugality		★		★			
Industry	★	★				★	★
Sincerity			★	★			★
Justice		★	★	★	★		
Moderation	★	★				★	
Cleanliness	★						
Tranquillity		★			★		
Chastity							
Humility		★					★

The End and the Beginning

BENJAMIN FRANKLIN "CONCEIV'D THE BOLD AND ARDUOUS PROJECT OF arriving at moral perfection" because he wanted to "live without committing any fault at any time." He undertook the course both for practical and spiritual reasons. In the end, he wrote that he "ow'd the constant felicity of his life, down to his 79th year" to the venture.

{ If you would not be forgotten
As soon as you are dead and rotten,
Either write things worthy reading,
Or do things worth the writing.}

I decided to follow Franklin's course of virtues as I stood in front of a magazine stand in a drugstore while I waited for a bus. I think that I had just bought some deodorant.

How did a Founding Father and a father too often lost get mixed up together in seeking moral perfection?

Before I get too far into such a weighty question, let me offer one more confession, one more mea culpa.

I lied. Again (for a guy who claims to treasure Sincerity so much, I seem to do that a lot).

I said in the beginning of this book that it would not contain any of the answers to life's fundamental questions. After thirteen-plus weeks of somewhat virtuous behavior, I might say that I was no closer to understanding the nature of the universe than I would have been had I watched continuous reruns of *Laverne and Shirley*. Go back to "The Preparations" and you'll see that I warned you.

The truth, however, is that there are some answers to the big questions—some gems of hidden knowledge—revealed within the pages of this book. Some you may have stumbled upon yourself, others you may need my assistance to uncover. Let's have a look at them together.

First, and this is probably the most obvious, I am no Benjamin Franklin. No course of virtue, no weekly lesson in moral perfection, is going to make me (or anyone else) into Citizen Ben. He was an extraordinary man with extraordinary gifts. I'm an average guy with heretofore undiscovered gifts (I can juggle, my pencil sketches are okay, and I make a pretty good cheesecake).

That does not mean that it was a mistake to follow Ben. He invited it, in fact. He wrote of his course:

> I hope, therefore, that some of my descendants may follow the example and reap the benefit.

Thus, though I may be no Franklin, in any sense of the word, for thirteen weeks I have felt his hand on my shoulder, guiding me through this course. I may not be him, now or ever, but after the thirteen weeks, I felt (and feel) a little closer to him. Actually, with all the false starts, mix-ups, and mistakes, the course took more than thirteen weeks, but what's a few weeks when you're seeking moral perfection?

Great Truth No. 2 is equally obvious. There is no such thing as moral perfection. Ultimately Franklin acknowledged as much. He wrote, in his own reflections on the course, that moral perfection was an impossible goal. Even in his failures, however, he saw no loss in the attempt. As a result of his course, he was a

> better and a happier man than I otherwise should have been if I had not attempted it; as those who aim at perfect writing by imitating the engraved copies, tho' they never reach the wished-for excellence of those copies, their hand is mended by the endeavor, and tolerable, while it continues fair and legible.

He ascribed various aspects of his success in life to the endeavor. He credited his good health to Temperance; to Industry and Frugality, his wealth. Sincerity and Justice won him "the confidence of his country" and his position as diplomat. To "the joint influence of the whole mass of the virtues," he attributed his "evenness of temper" and "cheerfulness in conversation."

{ *Be at war with your vices, at peace with your neighbors, and let every new year find you a better man.* }

Well, I can't give you that kind of lifetime assessment. Franklin had decades of hindsight with which to work. Of course, if you've stuck with me this long, I suppose you deserve some sort of postgame wrap-up.

This course began with a survey of my friends and family. It was meant to be a virtuous weigh-in, a starting point from which to assess the success of my journey to Benjamin Franklin's moral perfection. Now, after the completion of the course, had my quest yielded results? Would my family, friends, and coworkers notice any change? Would my quest to follow Franklin shine through? I decided another survey was in order.

You'll remember the survey of my mother and father, remembering as well that I am an only child. Well, despite their biased view of me even before I sought moral perfection, I decided to begin with them. Again via email, I asked them to answer my precourse survey, with another admonition to be honest. This was their response:

Can't say we have seen any changes, how can you improve perfection, ha???

It was certainly comforting to know that I had not diminished in their estimation, but that was hardly helpful as a postcourse debriefing.

I decided to move on to my colleagues. I was not hopeful of any endorsements of Franklin as a life-coach guru from this group. Their feelings about the entire enterprise were decidedly mixed. Perhaps "mixed" might even be a little Pollyannaish. I think they resented, ever so slightly, being part of a social experiment, and who could blame them? Notwithstanding that, I decided I had to be complete in my survey.

For the most part, the answers were what I expected. No real change noticed. No glow of virtue about me. Nothing morally perfect apparent in my character. One answer did, however, shock me.

When I asked one of my coworkers if my attempt to follow Ben had affected her in any way, she said, "Yes, as a matter of fact, it did."

I tensed. Was she about to say that I had driven her nuts? Or that I was a virtuous hypocrite? With a sense of foreboding, I asked, "How did it affect you?"

With the steely gaze developed over two decades of prosecuting some of our community's most dangerous people fixed on me, she said, "With all this talk of you trying to be a better person, I decided that I'd try to be a better person, too."

I was surprised. This was news to me. She had made no grand announcements of following Ben (or me) to moral perfection, so I had no idea I had inspired anyone. I was thrilled. "And you know what?" she continued.

"What?" I asked, cursing myself for an impetuous moment of self-congratulations and sensing the other shoe was about to drop.

"This trying to be a better person is %$#(*&! hard!"

So it is. So it is.

Next on my list of my interviewees were the girls. I had tried to involve them as little as possible in this whole endeavor because of their ages, but honesty is a gift of youth, and so I decided I might at least get some honest answers to questions about my character. Kids, as Art Linkletter reminded us, say the darndest things.

Simplifying the quiz was essential (would you want to ask a young child how good you were at Moderation?), so instead of asking them to rate me on the virtue of Temperance, for instance, I asked them to tell me how good I was at eating things that were good for me and not eating things that were bad for me. Darcy said simply, "You eat too much." Remember, I wanted honesty.

On Frugality, Harper said I spent too much; Darcy said, "I don't know what that means." On Silence, Harper felt I did say things about people but they were mostly nice, and she thought I was very honest when we talked about Sincerity. Tranquillity was difficult to explain, so I presented it this way: "When I spill a glass of milk or something like that, do I get angry and run around the house screaming or do I shake it off and say it's nothing?"

"Neither," said Harper. "You say, 'Oh crap.'" At least I had G-rated my expletive.

The rest of their answers were pretty straightforward, but on Order, Harper did mention that my closet was a mess. I found that very ironic given the fact that I had once lived in one.

It was on the animal question that I received perhaps the most honest and perceptive analysis. "If I were an animal, what would I be?" I asked (you would think I would have skipped over this one).

Harper thought about that for a moment and then replied, "I think of three animals: a hippopotamus, an elephant, and a rhinoceros."

Bracing myself, I asked, "Why?"

"Because," she answered, "they're gray and round."

She is her mother's daughter. Darcy, by the way, said anteater. I didn't have the courage to ask why.

Next to last was Chris Levan, he who had led me through this maze of virtues and ethics. Did he regard our efforts as successful, or was I a disappointment to him? We met, again, over a glass of wine at our local café.

"I enjoyed the experience," he said when I asked him about our thirteen weeks together. He explained that much of his professional life is dedicated to teaching the theory of virtuous behavior, but that my stumbling in the path of Benjamin Franklin was about how the unpredictability of life alters theory. "It was a good reminder," he continued, "that we can't control as much as we think."

I was curious to know if he had learned anything from the course. Or, more important, did he have any final words of wisdom for me? After a moment's thought, he nodded and said, "Two things.

First, anything worth doing takes more than a lifetime; therefore, we must be saved by hope. Second, none of us is as virtuous as we imagine ourselves; therefore, we must be saved by faith."

Not bad. I think that was worth the price of a glass of wine.

Finally, I moved on to Michelle. Though this was undoubtedly the most important interview, it was also the one I dreaded the most. It was she who designated me sloth, and it is she with whom I intend to spend the rest of my life. Couple this with the knowledge, which you now certainly also possess, that she does not sugarcoat the truth, and I admit that I was more than a little nervous.

"So," I told her, "I want to do that survey I did with you at the beginning of the course."

"Why?" That was not encouraging. I persevered, explaining my reasons, and she agreed, though I noted more than a hint of skepticism in her voice.

As I went through the virtues one by one, she described me in almost identical terms from our first interview. I ended each question by asking if she noticed any difference in me with respect to the virtue in question after the completion of the course. "No change," she'd answer each time.

Should I have expected her to notice a change after just thirteen weeks? Perhaps not, but a little encouragement might have been nice. I would have accepted a little insincerity at this point.

I had saved the animal question until the end for obvious reasons. Had I turned myself from sloth to stallion? There was only one way to find out. "You'll remember," I began, "that last time I asked you about what kind of animal you pictured me as and you replied"—I paused—"a sloth."

"And I stick by my answer."

"Wonderful," I replied.

"Wait," she said, hearing the disappointment in my voice. "I never did explain my answer. Sloth is not negative to me. When I think of a sloth, I think of a contented creature. I envision a sloth as happy, satisfied, and taking life one day at a time. I like sloths. I knew you were a sloth when I married you, and that's why I did."

Well, it wasn't stallion, but I'd take it.

So that's what others thought, but what about me? Did I actually improve through this course of virtues? You want the truth (admit it, you're thinking of Jack Nicholson right now, aren't you)?

Okay, let's start with the obvious. I began this course by, unfortunately, stepping on the scale. As you will recall, I was a bison-like 250 pounds. I willed myself, at the conclusion of the program, to step back on the scale (despite the setback in the doctor's office). To my surprise, I weighed 235 pounds.

That's not bad. Accounting for breaks, extra weeks, and delay, this thirteen-week course took about sixteen weeks. Unless my math is completely off, that's almost one pound lost per week. I think most nutritionists and diet experts would suggest that that is a healthy weight loss. And I did it without cutting out many of the foods that I enjoy. I might have been temperate after all.

Have there been other successes? Certainly my system of Order seems to have survived the entire program. I continue to monitor my emails and rid myself of unnecessary clutter with some regularity. That is not to say that I have become an Order guru. I have discovered, however, the virtue of organization. For that alone I am thankful to Mr. Franklin.

I BELIEVE I HAVE REINFORCED THE VALUE OF THE VIRTUES I THINK I already possessed in some measure: Tranquillity and Sincerity in particular (okay, Sincerity took a recent licking, and I almost slapped a defense lawyer the other day, but even Ben recognized that occasional transgressions would remain). Let's be frank, I needed some Tranquillity just to get through the course.

Those virtues that I thought would be the most elusive were indeed so; some seemed almost impossible. I had the most difficulty with the virtues that were more abstract, the least with the practical. That may be a reflection of my nature or the product of a limited imagination.

What about those big questions, the ones to which I claimed not to be seeking answers? I'd be lying if I said I started this only for the fun of eating less and not watching television. The truth is that I was inspired by the words of Walter Isaacson (which I quoted in the prologue of this book). Here, again, is what he wrote:

> It is useful for us to engage anew with Franklin, for in doing
> so we are grappling with a fundamental issue: How does one
> live a life that is useful, virtuous, worthy, moral and spiritually
> meaningful?[1]

When I read these words, I wanted the answer to the question. How *does* one live a life that is useful, virtuous, worthy, moral, and spiritually meaningful? I wanted to know for myself and for Benjamin Franklin and for all the people of the world who cry out for meaning and purpose in their lives. I wanted to know it because I think that the search for meaning is the one characteristic that binds all humanity: a desire to have purpose, to do good, to leave a legacy, to be remembered.

Remember the response that Peter Short (the former Moderator of the United Church) gives to people who ask him, "How can I make my life more meaningful?" He tells people to turn that "how" into a "why." He wants them to ask themselves, "*Why* do I want my life to be more meaningful?"

I sidestepped the question earlier, but I am ready to answer it, at least for myself, after these past thirteen-plus weeks. I mentioned my grandparents in Chapter 12, "Chastity." Their gravestone reads, "Life's Work Well Done." That's why I followed Franklin. I want someone, somewhere, after I have passed, to say of my time that it was "life's work well done."

BUT THAT'S NOT IT COMPLETELY. I DON'T THINK BEN FRANKLIN (NOR I) was seeking only personal satisfaction and aggrandizement. Despite criticism to the contrary, I believe that Franklin's course was, at its core, altruistic. Sure, he was trying to achieve personal success, but there was more to it than that. Franklin was trying to re-create himself as a person who valued community above self and charity over wealth. It seems to me that the fundamental aspects of his program of self-improvement, the foundation of virtuousness and the cornerstone of success in his mind, were found in his dictum in *Poor Richard's Almanack*: "The noblest question in the world is *What Good may I do in it?*"[2]

It is not a coincidence that Franklin suggested that he began each day of his course by asking himself this question. Selflessness, though not a specific virtue, is the beginning of understanding of self (that sounds almost profound; I must have stolen it from somebody else). The more we do for others, the better we feel about ourselves; the better we feel about ourselves, the more we are prepared to do for others. So . . . here is another "big" answer that I discovered—one more universal truth—from following Franklin. When I talked to Peter Short, I asked him why people want to sacrifice, to do good for others. His reply, a quote from Nelson Henderson, expresses this last truth more eloquently than I ever could. He said, "The true meaning of life is to plant trees, under whose shade you do not expect to sit."

Well, I don't know if I've planted any trees, but I have for thirteen weeks followed one of the world's greatest figures and felt his eye on me throughout the process. I have tried to be better and, in doing so, learned my last great truth.

Once I articulated *why* I wanted to be better—to have a more meaningful life— the *how* came easily. The secret to being better is to try. I may not have succeeded, but for these thirteen weeks I tried, and maybe, for these thirteen weeks, I was just a little more stallion than sloth.

Go with Ben.

{ *I should have no objection to go over the same life from its beginning to the end: requesting only the advantage authors have, of correcting in a second edition the faults of the first.* }

{FURTHER READING
ABOUT BENJAMIN FRANKLIN}

Benjamin Franklin is one of the most extensively researched and written about figures in American history. Indeed, the volume of material can be overwhelming, as I discovered in writing this book. For anyone interested in learning more about Franklin, here are some books that I found particularly useful:

The Autobiography of Benjamin Franklin
Edmund Morgan, *Benjamin Franklin* (New Haven and London: Yale University Press, 2002)
Walter Isaacson, *Benjamin Franklin: An American Life* (New York: Simon & Schuster, 2003)
Esmond Wright, *Franklin of Philadelphia* (Cambridge, Mass: The Belknap Press of Harvard University Press, 1986)
Page Talbott, ed., *Benjamin Franklin: In Search of a Better World* (New Haven and London: Yale University Press, 2005)
Willard Randall, *A Little Revenge: Benjamin Franklin and His Son* (Boston: Little, Brown and Company, 1984)

{NOTES}

Prologue

1. Isaacson, Walter, "Citizen Ben's Great Virtues," *Time* 162, no. 1 (July 7, 2003), www.time.com/time/2003/franklin/bffranklin.html.
2. Ibid.
3. Ibid.
4. McGee, Micki, *Self-Help, Inc.: Makeover Culture in American Life* (New York: Oxford University Press, 2007).
5. Salerno, Steve, *Sham: How the Self-Help Movement Made America Helpless* (New York: Crown, 2005).
6. Cicero, Marcus T., c. 106–43 BC.
7. Isaacson, "Citizen Ben's Great Virtues."
8. Dalton, Kathleen, *Theodore Roosevelt: A Strenuous Life* (New York: Alfred A. Knopf, 2002), p. 254.

The Preparations

1. Herman, Arthur, *How the Scots Invented the Modern World: The True Story of How Western Europe's Poorest Nation Created Our World and Everything in It* (New York: Crown Publishers, 2001), p. 64.

1. Temperance

1. Randall, Willard, *A Little Revenge: Benjamin Franklin and His Son* (Boston: Little, Brown and Company, 1984), p. 4.
2. "The Temperate Doctor," *Canadian Medical Association Journal* 162, no. 12 (June 13, 2000).
3. Ibid. See also Plato, *The Republic*, chapter 16, 430d.

2. Silence

1. Palatnik, Lori, and Bob Burg, *Gossip: Ten Pathways to Eliminate It from Your Life and Transform Your Soul* (Deerfield Beach, FL: Simcha Press, 2005).

4. Resolution

1. Dingfelder, Sadie F., "Solutions to Resolution Dilution," *Monitor on Psychology* 35, no. 1 (January 2004), www.apa.org/monitor/jan04/solutions.html.

5. Frugality

1. Morgan, Edmund S., *Benjamin Franklin* (New Haven and London: Yale University Press, 2002), pp. 22–23.
2. Isaacson, Walter, *Benjamin Franklin: An American Life* (New York: Simon & Schuster, 2003), p. 89.
3. Wright, Esmond, *Franklin of Philadelphia* (Cambridge, MA: The Belknap Press of Harvard University Press, 1986), p. 47.
4. David Brooks as quoted in Isaacson, *Benjamin Franklin: An American Life*, p. 90.

6. Industry

1. American Academy of Pediatrics, "Children, Adolescents, and Television," *Pediatrics* 107, no. 2 (February 2001), pp. 423–26, http://aappolicy.aappub lications.org/cgi/content/full/pediatrics;107/2/423.

8. Justice

1. Morgan, Edmund, "The End of His Pragmatism," in *Benjamin Franklin: In Search of a Better World*, Page Talbott, ed. (New Haven and London: Yale University Press, 2005), p. 300.
2. Ibid., p. 302.

9. Moderation

1. Houston, Alan, "The Man of Sense," *Humanities* 27, no. 1 (January/February 2006).
2. Ibid.
3. Isaacson, *Benjamin Franklin: An American Life*.

4. Isaacson, Walter, "What Benjamin Franklin Means to Our Times," in *Benjamin Franklin: In Search of a Better World*, p. 2.

11. Tranquillity

1. Moskowitz, Eva, *In Therapy We Trust: America's Obsession with Self-Fulfillment* (Baltimore and London: The Johns Hopkins University Press, 2001).
2. Ibid., p. 219.
3. Ibid., p. 220.
4. Ibid., p. 224.
5. Ibid., p. 237.
6. The workshop was delivered by Gerry J. Aubie of Chaleur Psychological and Counseling Services Inc. The handout "The Wear and Tear Syndrome of Stress" was adapted from D. A. Tubesing, "Stress Skills Workbook: A Structured Strategy for Helping People Manage Stress More Effectively" (Duluth, MN: Whole Person Associates, 1979), p. 7.

Conclusion

1. Isaacson, "Citizen Ben's Great Virtues."
2. *Poor Richard's Almanack 1738*.

{ABOUT THE AUTHOR}

Cameron Gunn is a prosecutor and author whose wife calls him a sloth. He lives in Fredericton, New Brunswick, Canada, with his wife, three children, and two mentally unhinged beagles. This is his first book.

Photo by Ginette Hannan